Corporate Strategy Toolkit

FAE (Business Lead

Corporate Strategy Toolkit

FAE (Business Leadership)

Published in 2011 by
Chartered Accountants Ireland
Chartered Accountants House
47-49 Pearse Street
Dublin 2

This publication is designed to provide accurate and authoritative information in regard to the subject matter covered. It is provided on the understanding that the Institute of Chartered Accountants in Ireland is not engaged in rendering professional services. The Institute of Chartered Accountants in Ireland disclaims all liability for any reliance placed on the information contained within this publication and recommends that if professional advice or other expert assistance is required, the services of a competent professional should be sought.

ISBN 978-1-907214-66-0

Typeset by Compuscript
Printed by GRAFO, S.A.

MIX
Paper from
responsible sources
FSC® C116691
FSC
www.fsc.org

Contents

Introduction

This Corporate Strategy Toolkit has been developed to provide you with a range of practical and applied exercises to enable you to apply the theory contained in the main text by Gerry Gallagher: *Corporate Strategy for Irish Companies* (2nd Edition, 2011). This is designed to enable you to develop and hone your strategic skills. The enclosed exercises include business-style exercises and practical exercises which will enable you to apply the theory. Business leadership is one of the key areas of assessment at the Final Admitting Exam (FAE), and this toolkit is designed to support you in the development of the necessary insights and skills. As noted in the toolkit, such skills are best developed by recalling the 3Ps (Practise, Practise, Practise!).

Good luck with your studies.

CHAPTER 1

Strategy Overview

Learning Objectives

The purpose of this chapter is to ensure that you have a clear understanding of the concept of strategy, its elements and processes. By the end of this chapter you should be able to:

- Identify and explain the specific elements of strategy.
- Explain the typical elements and levels into which strategy can be divided, and apply this in practice.
- Identify and explain the typical steps of the rational model of strategic planning.
- Appreciate different approaches to strategic planning and where these different approaches can be used.

The FAE Competency Statement includes the following learning outcomes:

- "Advise on the general objectives of strategic management and its role in developing the organisation"; and
- "Evaluate the role of leadership in developing corporate strategy and its limits with corporate culture."

Pre-reading

Read Chapter 1 of your main text: *Corporate Strategy for Irish Companies* by Gerry Gallagher (2nd Edition, 2011), hereinafter referred to as **Gallagher**.

Self-assessment

Before proceeding, think about your understanding of strategy, and any previous study of this area. Can you:

- Define the term strategy? (See **Section 1.1**)
- Identify the elements of strategy? (See **Section 1.2**)
- Distinguish the typical levels into which strategy in business can be classified? (See **Section 1.4**)
- Specify the steps in the traditional "rational" strategic model? (See **Section 1.5**.)
- Identify alternative approaches to strategy development? (See **Section 1.6**.)

1.1   STRATEGY DEFINITION AND OVERVIEW

Strategy is a course of action to achieve a particular objective. In simple terms, strategy is *where* you want to go to and *how* you plan to get there.

Exercise 1.1: Applying Strategy to Your Life – A Practical Example of Strategy

You have set yourself the objective of running the Belfast marathon this year. This is your objective.

Requirement: List 10 actions ('hows') that you will have to take to enable you to complete this (and remain motivated!).

(See SOLUTIONS at the end of this text.)

Your main textbook defines **corporate strategy** as "charting the future direction of a company by developing long-term goals that reflect stakeholders' interests and achieve sustainable competitive advantage" (***Gallagher***).

1.2   ELEMENTS OF STRATEGY

Another definition of strategy is given by Johnson, Scholes and Whittington, *Exploring Corporate Strategy,* 8th Edition (Prentice Hall, 2008). We can use this to identify the elements of strategy:

"Strategy in a changing environment is the *direction* and *scope* of an organisation over the *long-term*: which achieves advantage for the organisation through its configuration of *resources and competences*, to meet the needs of markets with the aim of fulfilling *stakeholder expectations*." (emphasis added)

Take a moment and review this definition, in particular the emphasised words:

- What do each of these elements/terms mean to you?
    - o   Direction of the business
    - o   Scope of the business
    - o   Long term
    - o   (Competitive) advantage
    - o   Resources (or competences)
    - o   Changing environment
    - o   Stakeholder expectations
- Can you think of a practical example of what these terms might mean for a client or company with which you are familiar?

Exercise 1.2: Applying Strategy Definition to Understand Aer Lingus's Strategy

Aer Lingus, under Willie Walsh during the late 1990s, decided to change from being a national carrier to a low-cost carrier airline. This set a *directional* change for Aer Lingus over the following years, and changed the *scope* of the airline. (By 'scope' is meant: 'what business are we in?'). This impacted on the areas of the business that Aer Lingus would operate in, and which fitted with the new definition of Aer Lingus as a low-cost carrier (e.g. short-haul, long-haul offerings were adapted (including business class, and 1st class), and freight and catering were no longer seen as appropriate and were discontinued).

Adopting a low-cost model defined the basis on which Aer Lingus would compete in the market place; low cost was the basis of its *competitive advantage*. The decision was influenced by the success of Ryanair, which had achieved significant growth in market share due to its adoption of a low-cost model. The emergence of Ryanair was the result of airline deregulation within the EU. Prior to this, airlines had operated in a heavily regulated market with national airlines competing in a cartel-like manner (with agreements of flight rates between airlines and the effective division of the market between them).

Any strategic decision or plan must consider both the *environmental fit* and *resource fit* of the strategy. In Aer Lingus's case, airline deregulation had resulted in a significant increase in competition, and reduced barriers to entry had resulted in significant lowering of fares. The new strategy sought to accommodate this new reality.

A strategy needs to consider the company's own *resources*, in this case: staff, fleet, finance, etc. Aer Lingus's financial position at this stage was weak, as it was loss-making. It was also affected by the banning by the EU of further government aid (due to competitive concerns). Consequently, it needed to adopt the change in strategy or face extinction.

In terms of staffing, the challenges were significant. Aer Lingus was heavily unionised, with inflexible work practices. A major change would be needed here if the new strategy was to succeed. There were also various stakeholders whose preferences needed to be considered. These ranged from the Government, which as the major shareholder might be concerned with job security (and its impact on marginal Dáil seats in the Dublin North constituency) and airline access, to the employees whose primary concern was job security and terms and conditions of service. In developing the strategy, Walsh sought to balance these conflicting expectations while ensuring the long-term success of the company.

Requirement:

- In the Aer Lingus example, clearly identify the elements emphasised in the Johnson, Scholes and Whittington definition of corporate strategy. (Avoid just paraphrasing the text. Can you think of practical examples of what each meant for Aer Lingus?)

- With the benefit of hindsight, was the choice of strategy successful?
- What challenges remain for Aer Lingus?

(See SOLUTIONS at the end of this text.)

Further Exercise: Consider how these points might apply to a key client or your employer.

Exam and Study Tip

Often, when presented with a problem like that in **Exercise 1.2**, you can think of many issues that face a particular company. A useful way of approaching this complexity is to ask what *five key issues* would 'keep you awake at night' if you were CEO or CFO?

By limiting yourself to (say) five high-level issues, you will bring a level of discipline to your decision-making, and avoid too many operational details, or at least ensure that you group these smaller issues into bigger problem areas. You should ask yourself why you have selected the items on your list. How you *justify* your selection of issues will be critical.

In order to consider and address exercises such as this you do not need to be an employee of Aer Lingus. Naturally, if you were an employee you would have the benefit of an *insider's information* and perspective, which is clearly not possible in this instance. Instead, the level of insight expected should be based on:

- information as presented in the exercise: you need to spend some time analysing and understanding the information, and why or how it is relevant or not; and
- 'general business knowledge'. In this respect you are encouraged to read the business press, e.g. the *Financial Times* and *The Economist* (both of which are available online www.ft.com and www.economist.com) in order to be fully conversant with current business issues.

1.3   STRATEGIC PLANNING

Strategic planning can be defined as determining our long-term goals and the policies that will ensure their achievement.

From this definition it should be clear that we are focusing on *long-term direction* and the relevant objectives and policies that will *guide* our achievement of these.

Approaching Strategic Problems – Analysing and Synthesising

In terms of thinking strategically, you should always ask yourself: where do I want to be in the long term? Starting with a clear picture of where you want to be is a powerful way to assist you with the day-to-day choices you make.

Strategic problems can appear to be challenging and 'woolly'. How do you know your analysis is complete, comprehensive and balanced? The process of analysing a strategy might be viewed in part as 'telling a story'. The 'story' (see the Aer Lingus example above) seeks to explain where we are and the key challenges we face (analysing). As we repeat the story to different stakeholders we gain a range of insights and views (synthesising) and the strategic story will become more complete.

You should try to avoid seeing strategic problems as having one cause or one answer – they are rarely so simple. Strategic problems are typically complex and require a balancing of perspectives. This is why we go through a series of discrete steps, each seeking to add to our understanding. By clarifying our objectives, analysing the situation and considering stakeholder perspectives, the external environment, and internal competencies, we build up a picture of where the organisation needs to go and can hopefully see a way to progress our organisation through the adoption of an appropriate strategy.

In this workbook it may appear that the strategic process is linear and sequential one with one step after another. In practice, the process is more iterative and you will likely have to revisit earlier steps a number of times.

Characteristics of Strategic Thinkers

As Chartered Accountants, you are expected to think strategically. This involves:

- **Being curious and questioning the status quo:** Is there a better way? Have we ever tried this?
- **Broadening your outlook:** To appreciate the issues from other perspectives.
- **Challenging the underlying assumptions:** What would have to change in order for us to do X?
- **Adopting flexibility in your thinking and approach:** What are the trade-offs? Don't just accept the immediate rebuff from colleagues and stakeholders.
- **Focusing on the future:** What can we do now to prepare for the future?

As you progress through this Toolkit, you will hopefully learn to be more *proactive*. Being proactive is essentially to be true to our nature, which is to be responsible (able to choose our response) rather than to be *reactive*. (Chapter 2 of ***Gallagher*** clarifies the role of the leader as well as the cultural dimension.)

The more time you spend practising your skills using the various tools in this kit, the stronger your insights and instincts. This is a key leadership skill. As with the development of any skill, the three "Ps" apply: Practise, Practise, Practise.

1.4   LEVELS OF STRATEGY

To explain strategy, we often classify strategy in business into three distinct levels:

- Corporate-level strategy;
- Business-level (or often Divisional/Strategic Business Unit SBU) strategy; and
- Operational strategy.

This hierarchy recognises that the strategy moves from 'big picture' to more detail as it cascades down through the organisation's hierarchy. *Management by objectives* is about setting clear objectives such that each part of the business (at each of the three levels: strategic or top management, middle management and operational staff) has objectives that are designed to contribute to the overall strategy. All of these objectives need to be fully aligned and consistent. This is not an easy thing to do but remains a challenge we must strive for.

It is very important that the strategies are aligned both horizontally and vertically. Otherwise, the various parts of the organisation will be "pulling" in different directions (termed '*sub-optimisation*'). (Vertical alignment is top down; horizontal alignment means all the departments must work together to achieve the corporate goals.)

Corporate-level strategy is concerned with the business as a whole and its long-term direction and scope ("what business are we in?"). Typically this is set by the Board.

In divisional organisations we are likely to have ***business-level strategies***. Each division's strategy (or strategic business unit) should be aligned to the corporate strategies. Each division may serve similar or different customers and segments, but should be contributing to the whole.

Operational strategy is the strategy at operational or functional level. Again, this should be aligned to the corporate and SBU strategies.

Exercise 1.3: Aer Lingus and the Three Levels of Strategy

Consider the case detail provided in **Exercise 1.2** about Aer Lingus and the decision to convert to a low-cost carrier. At what level of strategy is this decision? How does this decision impact the three identified levels of strategy?

- Corporate level
- Business (or divisional) level
- Operational level

(See SOLUTIONS at the end of this text.)

1.5   STRATEGY PROCESS OVERVIEW OF THE RATIONAL MODEL

The strategic planning process is typically (using the 'rational' model) divided into the following steps. These are explained in detail in your main text (see ***Gallagher,*** page 11).

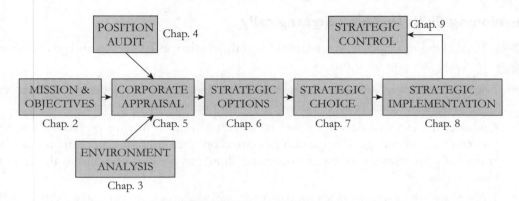

Figure 1.1: Overview of the Strategic Process

Exercise 1.4: Practical Personal Example

Think about your plan to run a marathon this year (see **Exercise 1.1**). Consider how each of the identified steps of the rational model can be used to assist you.

(See SOLUTIONS at the end of this text.)

Exercise 1.5: Practical Business Application

The Health Services Executive (HSE) is one of the largest single organisations in Ireland, with responsibility for the delivery of all aspects of the health system. To manage and develop such an immense and complex organisation requires careful and considered strategic business planning.

Requirement: Give examples of each stage of the rational model by reference to strategic planning in the HSE (Northern Ireland students may wish to refer to the National Health Service (NHS)).

  (a) Mission: What might the mission of the HSE be? (NI students use NHS.)
  (b) Objectives: What would the key objectives to achieve the mission be?
  (c) Environmental Analysis: What are the key environmental opportunities and threats facing the health system and the HSE/(NHS)?
  (d) Position Audit: What are the key competencies of the HSE/(NHS)? What are its strengths and weaknesses?
  (e) Corporate Appraisal (SWOT analysis): Can we complete a SWOT analysis?
  (f) Strategic Option Generation: What strategic options are available to tackle the identified issues?
  (g) Strategic Evaluation and Choice: What key choices will we make?
  (h) Strategic Implementation: How will this be rolled out? What (key performance indicators) KPIs do we have? What milestones have to be met?
  (i) Strategic Control: What measures might we use to monitor progress?

(See SOLUTIONS at the end of this text.)

Developing Skills to Think Strategically

In thinking strategically, you are looking at the challenges facing you and your business. In doing this you need to:

- Focus on a *medium- to long-term perspective*, rather than just an immediate and short-term one: try to stand back from the day-to-day and think of the long-term goals.

- Consider the external opportunities and threats arising from your *environment* and how you can take advantage of opportunities based on your strengths: here the focus is the fitting of your strategy to the environment: 'how can we best respond to the changed circumstances?'

- Understand the competencies and *strengths and weaknesses* of your organisation – this requires a 'hard-nosed' appraisal of your company relative to its competitors.

- Recognise that you have to cope with complexity while dealing with limited and incomplete information.

- Share ideas with colleagues to leverage on organisational capacity. Working with colleagues also enables you to test your developing strategy so that it does not create problems for other parts of the organisation later on.

1.6   ALTERNATIVE APPROACHES TO STRATEGY

Much of the management literature, including this toolkit, assumes a rational (step-by-step) approach to strategy. Alternative approaches, however, are also proposed in the literature. The range of different approaches reflects the complex and unstructured nature of strategy formulation and application. (See further reading in *Gallagher*, pages 14 to 24).

You should ensure you can distinguish between the following approaches to strategy development:

- **Rational approach:** This is a top-down approach to strategy, which is often criticised as being detached, periodic and inflexible. It can be seen to be imposed from the top.

- **Emergent approach:** This sees strategy as having a 'bottom-up element', learning from emerging trends rather than expecting the outcome to be in line with our plans. For example, we might adapt our marketing strategy based on feedback from our salespeople. This approach is particularly important in fast-changing environments.

- **Incremental approach:** Here, strategy is an extension of what went before and change occurs at the margin. This approach is popular in the public sector and works well in relatively stable environments.

Exercise 1.6: Possible Approaches to Strategy

Take the following organisations and consider which approach to strategy you might consider and why:

- Google
- Irish Rail
- A research institute (e.g. ESRI or equivalent)

For each organisation, which approach might work and why?

(See SOLUTIONS at the end of this text.)

SUMMARY – CHAPTER I

This chapter sought to provide you with an understanding of:

- The concept of strategy
- The three levels of strategy
- The steps in the strategic planning process
- Alternative approaches to strategy formulation

You should ensure you have satisfactorily achieved the learning objectives of this chapter before starting the next chapter.

REFERENCES

Gerry Gallagher, *Corporate Strategy for Irish Companies* (Chartered Accountants Ireland, 2nd Edition, 2011).
Johnson, Scholes and Whittington, *Exploring Corporate Strategy* (8th Edition, Prentice Hall, 2008).

CHAPTER 2

Vision, Mission, Objectives and Stakeholder Preferences

Learning Objectives

The purpose of this chapter is to ensure that you have a clear understanding of the hierarchy of objectives and an appreciation of stakeholder preferences. Before embarking on the development of your strategy, you need to know where you want to go! This chapter seeks to assist you in clarifying this.

At the end of this chapter you should be able to:

- Identify a possible hierarchy of strategic objectives.
- Explain the role of mission statements.
- Identify the typical elements of mission statements.
- Draft SMARTER objectives.
- Criticise and analyse a given set of objectives.
- Identify the different stakeholder preferences.
- Explain corporate social responsibility (CSR) and demonstrate how this impacts on an organisation's objectives and performance.

The FAE Competency Statement includes the following learning outcomes:

- "Advise on issues in relation to an entity's mission and objectives, ensuring consistency throughout."

Pre-reading

You should read *Gallagher*, Chapter 3.

Self-assessment

Before proceeding you might wish to reflect on your understanding of mission, objectives and stakeholder preferences from your previous study of this area. For example, in your earlier studies you have seen that business is normally seen as having a primary financial objective. This may conflict with the preferences of other stakeholders.

Can you:

- Identify a hierarchy of objectives? (See **Section 2.1**)
- Explain what a strategic vision is and how it might be used? (See **Section 2.2**)
- Explain the role of mission statements? (See **Section 2.3**)
- Specify the typical elements of mission statements? (See **Section 2.3**)
- Outline the suggested elements of objectives? (See **Section 2.4**)
- Describe the different stakeholder preferences? (See **Section 2.5**)
- Use stakeholder mapping to determine your response to the different stakeholder preferences? (See **Section 2.6**)
- Outline what corporate social responsibility is? (See **Section 2.7**)

In terms of our rational model of strategy, we are focusing on mission and objectives:

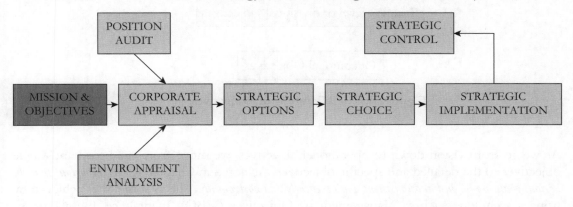

2.1   THE HIERARCHY OF OBJECTIVES

(See also *Gallagher*, Chapter 3.)

We can represent the various types of objectives (or goals) in the following hierarchy:

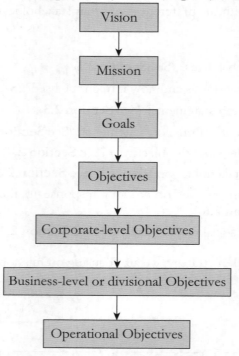

Figure 2.1: The Hierarchy of Objectives

As we go from vision down to operational objectives, we move from the broad and vague objectives to the detailed and specific objectives. As noted in Chapter 1, *it is important that the various goals are aligned and consistent, both vertically and horizontally*. This is sometimes achieved by using a technique such as Management by Objectives (MBO). In practice, the alignment process is complex and often difficult to achieve.

2.2   STRATEGIC VISION

A 'vision' is a picture of the future as in Martin Luther King's "I have a dream …" speech. A strategic vision allows the leader to present an alternative view or picture of the future and to challenge and motivate staff to buy into it. It can also express a statement of a core ideology.

Examples of effective visions in business include the vision Denis O'Brien offered his staff at ESAT Digifone of a youthful company setting out to compete with and beat Eircom. Avis, the car hire company expressed itself as: "We try harder", a total commitment to customer service (distinguishing itself from its main competitor, Hertz).

Exercise 2.1: A Personal Exercise on Vision

A common interview question is "*where do you see yourself in five years' time*?" Take five minutes to form a picture of what your answer to that might be.

Consider:

- What steps will you have to take to achieve this vision?
- What aspects of this picture attract you?
- How can you use this picture to motivate you on your way?

Hint: Remember if you really want to impact on someone's behaviour, you need to change people's vision (or picture) of themselves and their roles.

(See SOLUTIONS at the end of this text.)

2.3 MISSION

'Mission' is concerned with our long-term reason for existence. It may contain the:

- **Reason** or purpose for the company's existence;
- **Strategy** that we will follow, e.g. to focus on particular products or market segments only;
- **Values** (and culture) which underlie our operations; and
- **Policy** and behaviour standards that we will follow.

(The acronym **RSVP** may help you remember this.)

Anita Roddick, founder of The Body Shop, once said of her company's mission:

> "What is our mission? It's easy – We will be the most honest cosmetic company around. How will we do it? That's easy too – we will go diametrically in the opposite direction to the cosmetic industry."

Exercise 2.2: Analysing the Mission Statement

Can you analyse the Body Shop mission for the possible four elements?

(See SOLUTIONS at the end of this text.)

Exercise 2.3: Mission Statements

Here are more examples of mission statements:

- To make people happy
- Beat Coke

- Absolutely, positively overnight
- Undisputed leader in world travel

Can you suggest the company to which each mission statement refers?

(See SOLUTIONS at the end of this text.)

A mission, by definition, is open-ended (it is unlikely ever to be fully achieved) and general (contrasting with the specific nature of objectives). A mission can provide a focus and be a statement of the shared culture. Ideally, staff should partake in the development of the mission and it should not only be communicated, but also have resonance with all. Too often, mission statements are ignored and are not communicated, remaining unread on boardroom walls! To be effective, they should be applied in practice and lived.

Exercise 2.4: Some Questions on Your Organisation's Mission

- Does your organisation have a mission statement?
- Where would you find it?
- Do you believe in it?
- What changes might you make to it to make it more personal?

(See SOLUTIONS at the end of this text.)

Exercise 2.5: Personal Mission Statement

Stephen Covey in his book, *Seven Habits of Highly Effective People*, suggests that we should each have a personal mission statement. You might like to take the following exercise to assist you in determining some of the values that are important to you.

Imagine you are going to a funeral in 20 years' time. Imagine the church and the people (extended family, friends, workplace colleagues, other social activity contacts, etc.). Imagine the warm sense of purpose and sadness at the passing of a truly good person. (The person in the coffin is YOU.) What eulogies and words would you wish to be said about you by (take some time to think about this):

- A member of your extended family?
- A colleague at work?
- A friend?
- Someone from a social organisation in which you acted as a volunteer?

Consider: How might my priorities and actions need to change if my future behaviour is to merit these words?

(See SOLUTIONS at the end of this text.)

2.4 OBJECTIVES

The terms 'goal' and 'objective' are used interchangeably. Your main text, *Gallagher*, sees goals as being more qualitative, whereas objectives can be more quantitative in nature. This is a distinction that can get blurred in practice.

To motivate staff over the short, medium and long term, we need to convert our mission into practical *objectives*. Objectives should be set for all levels of the organisation, the departments and the individuals. To be effective, objectives should be **"SMARTER"**:

> **S**pecific – be precise
>
> **M**easurable – how will you know you have achieved it?
>
> **A**ttainable
>
> **R**ealistic
>
> **T**ime bound – by when?
>
> **E**xciting – (will the objective make me enthusiastic to achieve it)
>
> **R**eward linked – (but not just financial)

(To read further about SMARTER objectives, see *Slave to a Job, Master of your Career* by Sean McLoughney (Chartered Accountants Ireland, 2009)).

You might consider your objective of running a marathon in **Exercise 1.1** and consider how each of these elements might be reflected in the objective.

Some Reflections on Objectives

In determining and agreeing objectives, one needs to recognise that balance is needed:

- Primary (e.g. financial) versus secondary objectives:
  - o Primary objectives should take precedence over secondary objectives.
- Corporate objectives should determine unit objectives for individual departments (horizontal alignment).
- The need to balance financial versus non-financial objectives: non-financial objectives can sometime override financial ones. (Can you think of an example?)
- Long-term versus short-term objectives, e.g., in coping with the economic downturn, we may focus on short-term savings:
  - o cutting back on staff investment such as training;
  - o reducing advertising to save money; and
  - o reducing R&D expenditure.

All of these are likely to impact in the long-term; however, priorities need to be identified and expressed. Trade-offs need to be detailed and clarified rather than ignored.

Exercise 2.6: Personal Example

In terms of your own life:

- Identify the key (say four to five) roles that you have.
- For each role identify the key objectives.
- How will you achieve balance between them?

(See SOLUTIONS at the end of this text.)

Exercise 2.7: Work Example – Annual Appraisal Goals

- What goals did you agree to as part of your annual appraisal for this year?
- Do you monitor your progress?
- What actions can you take to address any issues which have arisen?

(See SOLUTIONS at the end of this text.)

Exam Tip: Possible Examination-Style Question

 You might be asked to define a possible mission and objectives for the company in a particular case. Alternatively, you might be asked to critique a given strategy or mission for the organisation.

Hint: In doing this, reflect on the typical elements of a mission statement as outlined above or, in the case of objectives, consider whether they meet the SMARTER criteria.

Additionally, you should consider balance. Do the objectives or mission balance such issues as:

- Long term versus short term?
- How risk is considered and managed?
- Financial versus non-financial criteria?
- Environmental considerations?
- Ethical issues?

Conflict between the demands of secondary objectives can be dealt with by:

- rational evaluation – analysing the alternatives, one by one;
- bargaining between managers resulting in a satisfactory rather than an optimal result; and
- addressing goals in turn or periodically.

(See **Exercise 2.10** below, which develops some of these themes.)

2.5   STAKEHOLDER PREFERENCES

Stakeholder mapping is a useful tool to determine our response to the different stakeholder preferences. ***Gallagher*** suggests using the Balanced Scorecard (see page 91 onwards).

Stakeholders cover shareholders, managers, staff, customers, suppliers, financiers, government, local lobby groups, etc. Each group will have its own preferences, biases and priorities. Consider any organisation with which you are familiar and you can easily see the differing perspectives.

2.6   STAKEHOLDER PREFERENCES AND STAKEHOLDER MAPPING

From your studies to date (e.g. in finance), it should be apparent that managing any organisation involves conflicts between the various stakeholders, given their varying interests. The job of management is to seek to balance these conflicts in such a way that the result is *optimal* for the organisation *as a whole*. This is not an easy thing to do.

The power of the different stakeholders can result in sub-optimal outcomes. Typically, we assume that shareholder interests predominate. However, this may not always apply in reality as management's self-interest or strong union activity, for example, can undermine this. Eircom's management was criticised post-privatisation for focusing on its own interests and not that of its shareholders.

Key questions to ask:

- Who are the key stakeholders in an organisation with strong trade union activity?
- Where do they get their power?
- Consider the impact of ownership (political interference occurs in state-owned companies). How might privatisation affect this?

Exercise 2.8: Business Example – Different Objectives

How would the interests and expectations differ between the following four categories of employees working in a state-funded hospital?

(a) Hospital consultants
(b) Hospital administrators/finance department staff
(c) Hospital porters
(d) Nurses

(See SOLUTIONS at the end of this text.)

Stakeholder Mapping Tool

Mendelow has developed a useful tool (matrix) to analyse the stakeholder power and interest known as 'stakeholder mapping'. This recognises that each stakeholder group will have different power and interest. It also suggests that the location of the stakeholder will determine a different response from the organisation.

This is represented in **Figure 2.2** below.

	Low Interest High	
Low	Minimal effort	Keep Informed
Power		
High	Keep Satisfied	Key Players

Figure 2.2: Mendelow's Matrix

Exercise 2.9

The planned Shell efforts to bring gas onshore in County Mayo have been in the media over the last few years. Consider the various stakeholders (public at large (e.g. in Dublin), Mayo County Council, the Government, local community, and environmental activists) and decide in which segment you would place them and why.

(See SOLUTIONS at the end of this text.)

2.7 CORPORATE SOCIAL RESPONSIBILITY

(See *Gallagher*, Chapter 4, which covers the whole area of governance, ethics and corporate social responsibility (CSR).)

The modern business environment expects that some consideration will be given to CSR and thus this can impact on objectives. You will study professional and business ethics separately in your FAE studies. It is worth considering how corporate social responsibility might be considered within the objective-setting process.

Traditionally, there are two conflicting views: academics like Milton Friedman argue that the function of the business is to make money for the shareholders and anything that distracts from this is unjustified. An alternative view argues that a business does not have an existence solely to make money but owes a responsibility to the environment in which it operates.

Consider why your employer might:

- Sponsor a local charity fundraiser?
- Allow staff time off to work for free for a charity?
- Act in an ethical manner beyond what the law requires?
- Pay redundancy (or maternity benefits) beyond what the law requires?

Criteria for Assessing our Ethical Behaviour

The following short ethical checklist (from the Rotary organisation) is useful to evaluate your (or your organisation's) behaviour:

- Is it legal (to the letter of the law or the spirit of the law)?
- Is it truthful?
- Is it fair to all concerned?
- Is the behaviour defendable (to your mother, for example)?

In the modern environmentally sensitive world, an additional question can be added:

- Is it sustainable?

(This is similar to the list in the ethical framework on page 119 in *Gallagher*.)

Exercise 2.10: Minco Mining plc

Minco Mining plc is planning to establish a mine in a remote corner of Donegal which is sparsely populated. The area is noted for its scenic beauty. The mine operation has received planning permission from Donegal County Council following a period of significant lobbying of local politicians. Given rising global mineral prices, the mine is expected to be profitable and to generate employment in an area with little job potential and with a history of high emigration. The mine is expected to generate significant waste, but the company is confident that the waste arising, while not particularly attractive, will not contaminate the local water supply. Local environmentalists and farmers oppose the development. Minco's mission as stated in their most recent annual report is to "maximise shareholder wealth at all times and to act in an environmentally ethical manner".

Requirement:
1. Comment on the mission as outlined.
2. Use the Rotary ethical checklist above to analyse Minco's behaviour.

(See SOLUTIONS at the end of this text.)

SUMMARY – CHAPTER 2

This chapter has sought to provide you with a clear understanding of:

- A hierarchy of different objectives.
- The role of vision.
- The mission statement and its elements (RSVP).
- The elements which should be contained in objectives (SMARTER).
- Stakeholder preferences (and stakeholder mapping).
- The role of corporate social responsibility and its impact on our objectives.

You should ensure you have satisfactorily achieved the learning objectives of this chapter before starting the next chapter.

REFERENCES

Johnson, Scholes and Whittington, *Exploring Corporate Strategy* (8th Edition, Prentice Hall, 2008).

Stephen Covey, *Seven Habits of Highly Effective People* (Franklin Covey, 2003).

Sean McLoughney, *Slave to a Job, Master of your Career* (Chartered Accountants Ireland, 2009).

CHAPTER 3

Environmental Analysis

Learning Objectives

The purpose of this chapter is to ensure that you have a clear understanding of the tools to analyse the environment and the threats and opportunities which the changing environment poses for organisations. Developing your skills to 'read the environment' is a strategic skill. To do this, we will show you a range of models/tools to undertake this analysis.

After studying this chapter you should be able to:

- Distinguish different levels of the business environment.
- Analyse the environment using PEST/PESTEL analysis in order to evaluate the differing factors impacting on the organisation.
- Analyse a business market's competitive forces using Porter's Five Forces model.
- Identify your competitors and their potential strategies.
- Appreciate the insights from Porter's Diamond model at an international level.
- Use a suggested three-step approach to analysing the environment.

The FAE Competency Statement includes the following learning objective:

- "Identify current and future issues (including ICT, market forces and globalisation) driving change in a given sector using appropriate techniques."

Pre-reading

You should read *Gallagher*, Chapter 5.

Self-assessment

Before proceeding you might wish to reflect on your awareness of possible models to analyse the environment. We will present this at three levels:

- The industry (or micro) level
- The macro level (economy-wide view)
- The global perspective

Can you:

- Distinguish the different business environments? (See **Section 3.2**)
- Apply the PEST (or PESTEL) model to evaluate the different factors (opportunities and threats) impacting on an organisation? (See **Section 3.3**)
- Apply Porter's Five Forces model at an industry level to assess the competitive forces in an industry? (See **Section 3.4**)
- Use Porter's Diamond model to assess global developments, opportunities and threats? (See **Section 3.5**)
- Conduct an analysis of the threats and opportunities facing an organisation?

In terms of our rational model of strategy, we are focusing on the environment, as represented below:

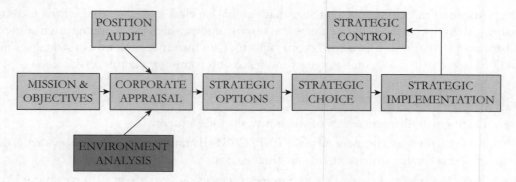

3.1   INTRODUCTION

Understanding the environment is a key challenge in terms of ensuring that we recognise:

- the threats to a business that a changing environment poses; and
- the opportunities that changes to the environment can create.

Reading the Environment is Not Easy!

Exercise 3.1: Reading the Environment

Try this simple exercise: Slip your wristwatch into your pocket. Then, from memory, draw a picture of the watch face.

Take a minute to do so.

Draw your answer here:

Some reflections

Understanding the environment is not easy because:

- typically we are not good at taking time to read the changes that are going on;
- the environment is complex and the interdependencies are hard for any one person or group of experts to appreciate and understand;
- our recent experience tends to colour our expectations of the future; and
- the level of expertise needed to read and understand the changes is often not available.

(See SOLUTIONS at the end of this text.)

3.2   DIFFERENT LEVELS OF BUSINESS ENVIRONMENT

Tools to Analyse the Environment

Three broad approaches (or tools) or levels are suggested to analyse the environment:

- At a *macro level* PEST (or PESTEL) can be used to evaluate the particular issues impacting on the environment and organisation.
- At an *industry level* we can use Porter's Five Forces model to understand the competitive forces at work.
- At an *international* or *global level* Porter's Diamond can be used to explain indicators of possible long-term success internationally.

3.3   PEST/PESTEL ANALYSIS

Economy-wide/Macro Analysis Using PEST

(See *Gallagher*, pages 164 onwards.)

Exercise 3.2: Brewing Industry Exercise

You have recently qualified as a Chartered Accountant and have been asked to undertake a PEST/PESTEL analysis of a local brewery based in your home town. Take 10 minutes to undertake this analysis.

Some reflections

- The list of issues is potentially endless.
- You are not expected to be an expert on the brewing industry.
- A key skill at this stage is to brainstorm your ideas:
  - o Remember that all ideas are good ideas; don't discount the craziest idea – ask how it might work/be made relevant.
  - o Try to think 'outside the box'; consider what is not relevant as well as what is. Can you see patterns from other industries that are relevant?
  - o As with any skill, the three Ps apply (Practise Practise Practise).

Try using this model with your clients; it will assist you in honing your skills.

(See SOLUTIONS at the end of this text.)

Exercise 3.3

Carry out a PEST analysis on the opportunities and threats to your career as a Chartered Accountant.

(See SOLUTIONS at the end of this text.)

Assessing Your Ideas about the Environment: A Three-step Approach

Developing a comprehensive list of ideas using a tool like PEST is helpful, but is only the start. A suggested approach to developing your ideas is given below:

1. *Identify the issues that are likely to impact on your business going forward*

   - What technologies are in other industries that might be used to create competitive advantage?
   - What are our potential competitors on the other side of the world doing?
   - How are our customers' needs and preferences changing?

Ideally, you should have as broad a sweep of issues and areas as possible. No one person will have all the answers, so the wider the consultation you undertake the better. You should also challenge the assumptions on which the issues are identified and how they are assumed to continue. Many projections are simply an extension of the past.

Some actions to assist you might include:

- considering the pros and cons;
- trying to build a picture of the future which might be very different from the past;
- being flexible and willing to revise and adapt your thinking to reflect the feedback and opinions shared; and
- looking at the issues systemically: how do the various factors interact and if there are any other knock-on factors.

2. *Assess the future impact on your business of the identified issue*

How much will the particular change impact on us (in terms of sales, profit and market share) and by when (by year)? It is unlikely that we can get an exact fix on this and we may wish to look at a range of alternatives or carry out some sensitivity analysis or scenario planning. In practice, you will wish to talk to a range of experts and colleagues to assist you. Colleagues in the marketing department, external experts and research reports can help. You cannot assume that you can make decisions without your competitors responding. Examine how they have performed in the past – this often is an indicator as to how they may react next time.

3. *Determine your response*

Having identified and assessed the issues creating threats and opportunities, the key issue is how these can be taken advantage of. Your response could include:

- **Doing nothing**, because you are happy with the change or need more time to assess it.
- **Seize the opportunity** and adapt your business to the changed circumstances (e.g. Body Shop and the green agenda).
- **Fight the change** through lobbying or otherwise (e.g. National Rifle Association in the US).
- **Consider alternative options** such as developing a potential alternative product (some saccharine manufacturers developed alternative sweeteners prior to it being banned).
- **Leave a market** that is no longer seen as profitable or attractive (e.g. asbestos mining or tobacco sectors might be seen as unattractive).

This process should not be a one-off exercise but an ongoing one. Remember the words of Andy Grove of Intel: "only the paranoid survive"!

> ### Exercise 3.4: Another PEST Exercise
>
> Carry out a PEST analysis to identify the key issues facing **Specky for Eyes** (see Case Study in **Appendix 1**). For each issue identified, state why you believe this is important and identify possible sources of information for each.
>
> (See SOLUTIONS at the end of this text.)

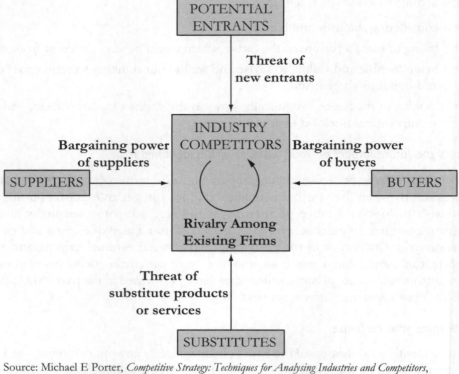

Source: Michael E Porter, *Competitive Strategy: Techniques for Analysing Industries and Competitors*, New York, The Free Press, 1980.

Figure 3.1: The Five Forces Model

3.4   INDUSTRY ANALYSIS/PORTER'S FIVE FORCES

Analysing the Environment at an Industry Level: The Five Forces Model

Moving from an economy-wide view or macro view to an industry level, we want to understand the competitive forces operating at an industry level. Porter's Five Forces model is a useful tool here.

Exercise 3.5: Using Five Forces Analysis

(Before doing this exercise you may wish to read **Gallagher** (pages 173 onwards).)

Taking the airline industry, use the Five Forces Model to analyse the impact of airline deregulation.

Background detail Prior to deregulation, the market can be analysed as follows:

- *Barriers to entry* Historically, this was a controlled (regulated) industry with national airlines controlled by governments under IATA regulations. Agreements between countries were on a bilateral basis with an effective carve-up of markets. Ability to enter the market was thus severely restricted. The lack of available finance and access to airport slots also acted as barriers to entry.

- *Competitive rivalry* The market operated as an effective cartel with 'limited/controlled' rivalry. Travel was seen as exclusive and costly.

- *Power of suppliers* Major suppliers were airplane manufacturers (several players), competition amongst fuel suppliers was present, finance from banks was limited but available. The last 20 years have seen the emergence of two main airplane suppliers, Boeing and Airbus. Aircraft leasing has made access to planes easier.

- *Power of customers* Traditionally, except for the large tour operators who could buy in bulk, customer power was weak and fragmented.

- *Threat of substitutes* Traditionally, airline flights were exclusive and expensive compared to substitutes such as boat, train or car.

Deregulation represents the process of removal of legal and other practices that have hampered competition. This process began in the US in the 1980s and resulted in the creation of new low-cost operators such as People Express and South West Airlines. In the late 1980s, the EU began to adopt similar practices in Europe.

Requirement: Analyse how the deregulation of this industry would impact on the Five Forces outlined above.

Based on your analysis, what are the key changes which have taken place?

Some reflections

This example shows the impact of deregulation on an industry. Porter argues that the forces explain the overall level of profitability of an industry. A key challenge for a business is to seek to create barriers to entry and other actions to strengthen their market position. See *Gallagher* for how this might be done (e.g. using patents and trademarks might be one example of a barrier to entry). Another key change which impacts on the market is changes in technology which can be quite disruptive. Consider the impact of the Internet on the airline industry example above.

(See SOLUTIONS at the end of this text.)

Exercise 3.6

Use Porter's Five Forces to consider possible impacts on the accounts preparation service in an accountancy practice.

(See SOLUTIONS at the end of this text.)

3.5   AN INTERNATIONAL PERSPECTIVE: USING PORTER'S DIAMOND

(See *Gallagher*, pages 159 onwards.)

Having considered the environment at a macro and micro (industry) level, we turn to the global perspective. Again, Porter's ideas can assist us. He argues that in a globalised world the economies that will succeed need to focus on four separate but interrelated elements, as represented in the diagram below. This model can be used by governments to guide them in creating an attractive environment and also by companies seeking to determine where they should invest internationally. The four elements are:

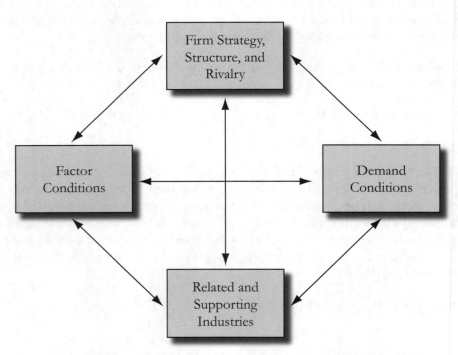

Source: Michael E. Porter, *The Competitive Advantage of Nations*, London, Macmillan, 1998.

Figure 3.2: Porter's Diamond

Factor conditions are divided into:

- **basic** (those that a country is endowed with, such as minerals, oil, gas, land, water, etc.); and

- **advanced**, such as educated workforce (and supporting education infrastructure), research and development capacity and infrastructure.

It is the advanced factors (not the basic factors) that achieve competitive advantage.

Michael Porter argues (regarding **demand conditions**) that those countries with a large local demand can build up a successful business model with economies of scale before expanding overseas. Home markets set fundamental parameters, such as market segments, degree of sophistication and rate of innovation. Early saturation of a local market will encourage the development of export markets. Porter identifies the UK horticulture industry as producing advantages for the UK in the area of garden tools, etc. This is based on the strong UK interest in gardening.

Firm strategy and rivalry Porter argues that a competitive home market will tend to build strengths which will be supportive of international expansion. For example, the Japanese electronic industry innovates and imitates rapidly. Such rivalry hones skills, and this capacity should enable them to hone a product before selling to an international market.

Related and supporting industries are critical to success. For example:

- The supporting legal and accounting services are important to the IFSC as well as an appropriate IT infrastructure and oversight.
- Silicon Valley benefits from strong university links and venture capital.
- The Italian clothing industry is supported by design workshops, dye industry and textile innovation.

Exercise 3.7: Applying Porter's Diamond

You have been asked to advise IDA Ireland (or Invest NI) on five actions that might be taken to attract inward investment. Use the ideas from Porter's Diamond to help you.

List your actions below:

1.

2.

3.

4.

5.

(See SOLUTIONS at the end of this text.)

Exercise 3.8: Case Study Example

(See **BWF Case – Exercise 1** in the Black & White Foods Case Study at **Appendix 2**.)

Understanding Your Competitors and Their Strategies

Most competitors do not always express their plans openly. We can find out what is happening in the market through:

- Publicly available information
- Past management and approaches
- Experience in the marketplace from front line staff such as sales people. What are competitors' strengths and weaknesses? What do our customers say about the opposition?
- Our own experience and hunches.

Exercise 3.9: Analysing Your Competitors

- Who are your employer's main competitors?
- What are the competitive pressures that are impacting on the business?
- How is your employer responding to this?
- What are the long-term implications of these pressures?

(See SOLUTIONS at the end of this text.)

CONCLUSION

This text has provided you with a set of tools you might use to analyse the environment of a particular company. This recognises three levels of analysis:

- the industry level (using Porter's Five Forces);
- the macro level (using PEST analysis); and
- the global level (using Porter's diamond model).

The purpose of this process is to assist you in identifying the *threats* and *opportunities* which the changing environment poses.

Not all threats are immediately obvious, as reflected in the Japanese idea of 'boiled frog syndrome'. (If you put a frog on a hot frying pan, he will hop off immediately, remaining unharmed. However, if you put a frog into cold water and increase the heat gradually, he will swim around, unaware of the increase in temperature until it is too late.) The message is clear: change can creep up on you, and you may not notice until it is too late. Thus, "only the paranoid survive". Your focus should always be to focus on those aspects over which you have some control and influence.

SUMMARY – CHAPTER 3

This chapter sought to provide you with different approaches to analysing the environment:

- Three steps to analyse the environment.
- Using different approaches to analyse the environment:
    o Macro level, using PEST/PESTEL to consider the issues impacting on the organisation.
    o Industry level, using Porter's five forces to understand the competitive forces at work.
    o Global level, using Porter's diamond.
- Analyse a company's competitors.

The aim of using these tools is to be able to realistically assess the opportunities and threats facing an organisation.

You should ensure you have satisfactorily achieved the learning objectives of this chapter before starting the next chapter.

REFERENCES

Michael Porter, *Competitive Advantage of Nations* (Simon & Schuster, 1998).
Michael Porter, *Competitive Advantage* (The Free Press, 1985).

CHAPTER 4

Position Audit: Evaluating an Organisation's Strategic Capability

Learning Objectives

The purpose of this chapter is to ensure that you have a clear understanding of the tools used to analyse an organisation's strengths and weaknesses which allow us to gain competitive advantage. In Chapter 2 we discussed the mission and objectives of an organisation. In Chapter 3 we examined the external environment. Now we examine resources and weaknesses/competencies.

Having covered the chapter you should be able to:

- Assess an organisation's strengths and weaknesses/core competencies;
- Analyse an organisation's tangible and intangible resources using appropriate models;
- Explain the role of benchmarking in assessing a company's strengths (and thus its competencies);
- Critically evaluate the organisation using the value chain.

The FAE Competency Statement includes the following learning outcome:

- "Assess the impact of these opportunities on the organisation and its strategy, its current position and objectives."

This is relevant to Chapter 4 and Chapter 5.

Pre-reading

You should read *Gallagher*, Chapter 6.

Self-assessment

Before proceeding, reflect on your knowledge of possible strategic tools or models to analyse a business in order to determine its strengths and weaknesses.

Can you:

- Evaluate a company's tangible and intangible resources using appropriate models? For example:
  - o   the 9M model;
  - o   the product life cycle; and
  - o   the BCG matrix. (See **Section 4.2**)
- Analyse a company's basic core competencies? (See **Section 4.1**)
- Understand the role of benchmarking and how it can be used? (See **Section 4.3**)
- Critically evaluate a company's value chain? (See **Section 4.4**)
- Assemble and analyse a company's strengths and weaknesses?

In terms of our rational model of strategy, our focus is now on the position audit:

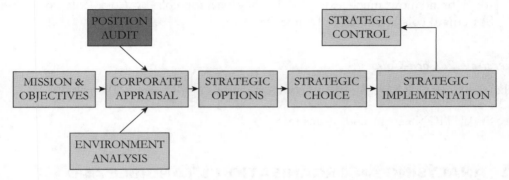

4.1   INTRODUCTION

Before determining our strategic options we need to understand our strengths and weaknesses, as these contribute to our 'core competencies' on which we establish competitive advantage in the marketplace. By understanding our strengths and weaknesses, we can hopefully take advantage of threats and opportunities facing us.

Exercise 4.1: Personal Assessment Exercise

Take any area of your life (work, home life, hobbies, sport, etc.) and **assess** your key strengths and weaknesses. Be as honest as you can.

Hint: Remember your strengths can become weaknesses and weaknesses can be strengths.

(See SOLUTIONS at the end of this text.)

A Practical Approach to Assessing Strengths and Competencies

Useful questions to ask are:

- What is it that we are good at as a business that is *valued* by our customers? This may be different from what we tend to emphasise as a business.

- Who are our customers and what are their priorities and preferences? How are these changing? Customer focus groups and market research can assist here. Customers are often the best source of new ideas.

- Are these strengths, in areas where we have *leadership* or competitive advantage over our competitors, that are hard to copy and imitate? Can we protect our lead through copyright and patents or other methods?

- Are our strenghts in areas where customers are willing to pay a premium? For example, for a brand how much extra would they pay for cola by Coca-Cola compared to St Bernard cola brand (from Dunnes Stores)?

Exercise 4.2: Coca-Cola

What are Coca-Cola's strengths and competencies using the criteria above?

(See SOLUTIONS at the end of this text.)

4.2   ANALYSING AN ORGANISATION'S TANGIBLE AND INTANGIBLE RESOURCES

To enable us to assess our strategic situation we can use a number of tools:

- 9M checklist
- Product Life Cycle
- BCG Matrix

We will examine practical examples/exercises of each model.

Position Audit Example: The 9M Checklist

The 9M checklist is a 'quick and dirty' (i.e. pragmatic) tool to analyse the business by examining the following nine resources:

- Materials (suppliers/resources)
- Manpower resources
- Machinery
- Money (finances/funding)
- Management resources
- Market standing/share

- Makeup (e.g. supply chain)
- Methods and processes
- Management Information Systems (MIS)

Exercise 4.3: Practical Application of the 9M Model

Take an organisation you know (or a client) and assess its strengths and weaknesses against the above list.

(See SOLUTIONS at the end of this text.)

Exercise 4.4: Applying the 9M Model to Ryanair

Analyse Ryanair using the 9M Model:

- Material resources
- Manpower
- Machinery
- Money/finances
- Management resources
- Market standing
- Makeup/supply chain
- Methods and processes
- MIS

(See SOLUTIONS at the end of this text.)

Weaknesses of the 9M Model

The model's weakness is that it does not consider:

- Customer preferences and how they may be changing.
- No weightings are given to each area. (Ryanair's ability to offer low-cost routes is a key factor.)
- Risks: What are the key risks? (Safety is a key issue for Ryanair.)

Nonetheless, as noted already, it may be viewed as a useful 'quick and dirty' starting point.

Exercise 4.5: Obtaining Information

You are going for a job in an industry you are not familiar with. What sources of information might you be able to use?

(See SOLUTIONS at the end of this text.)

Sourcing and Assessing Information

Information can be classified into internal (management reports and accounts, marketing reports) and externally available (published accounts, media reports, etc.) How much reliance would you place on these sources? What other sources might you use? Who else could you talk to?

Applying the Product Life Cycle

Read *Gallagher*, pages 287 onwards before proceeding.

The Product Life Cycle (PLC) is a tool to analyse product ranges and to recognise the impact of time. All products eventually die. Newspapers have been around since the 18th Century – they are showing signs of being in the decline phase of their life.

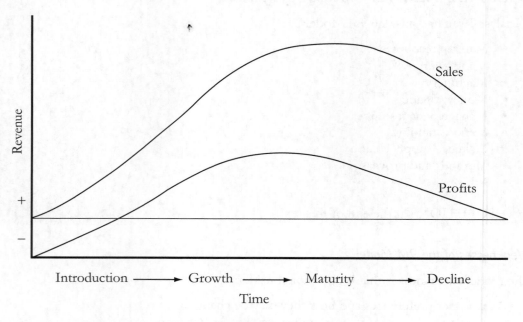

Figure 4.1: Product Life Cycle

Exercise 4.6: Product Life Cycle

Assume you are working in the television manufacturing division of an electronics company. Where in the product life cycle (introduction, growth, maturity and decline) might you place the following products:

- Black and white television
- Digital TV
- Flat screen TV
- Internet broadcasting
- 3D TV
- Interactive TV

(See SOLUTIONS at the end of this text.)

Other things to consider:

- Where do you think you would wish to concentrate your efforts and resources?
- What are the key skills needed for each stage in the life cycle in terms of product, price, promotion and place?

Exercise 4.7: PLC Messages

What are the three key insights of the Product Life Cycle (PLC)?

(See SOLUTIONS at the end of this text.)

Exercise 4.8: PLC Question – Mature Stage

As a marketing manager, what do you think are the techniques you might use to extend the maturity stage of a product's life cycle?

(See SOLUTIONS at the end of this text.)

Applying the Boston Consulting Group (BCG) Matrix

(Read *Gallagher* pages 322 onwards.)

The BCG matrix can be used to assess the organisation's product portfolio. The matrix analyses each product or product group on the following matrix:

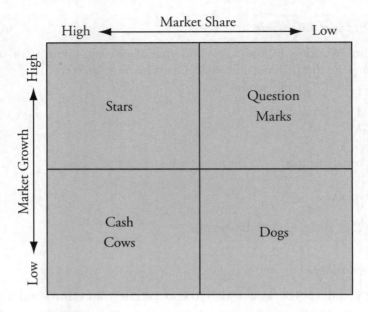

Figure 4.2: The Boston Consulting Group (BCG) Matrix

Exercise 4.9: BCG Application

- What issues would arise if all products were either stars or question marks (problem children)?
- Alternatively if all products were either cash cows or dogs?

(See SOLUTIONS at the end of this text.)

Key messages of the BCG matrix include:

- We need to have a balanced portfolio of products.
- Products will progress over time from question mark (introduction phase) to star (growth phase), cash cow (maturity) and dog (decline).
- Sufficient cash cows are needed to fund the developing products as these are cash generative; question marks and stars are cash absorbers.

4.3   BENCHMARKING

(Read *Gallagher*, pages 214 onwards.)

Benchmarking means having externally compiled independent data which compares information across an industry or process. It is a useful source of information in this process. (Ryanair regularly benchmarks itself against its competitors on a number of key criteria.)

Benchmark data needs to be compiled in a consistent manner and by:

- industry (to capture this data we may need to use an independent consultant to assist us);
- process (e.g. manufacturing process, distribution process, airline check-in process); and
- within a company (comparing divisions or subsidiaries).

It is useful to have independent 'hard' measures to challenge a particular situation. These enable us to justify our claim to be superior in a particular area rather than doing so subjectively. In assessing a health system you might wish to compare:

- average waiting times for a procedure;
- average cost per procedure; and
- effective outcomes of the procedure.

Of course, having such information is only the start. You need to understand *why* the process may be costing more. Perhaps this reflects superior customer service or a way of achieving long-term superior performance. A risk of any benchmark process is that all organisations become the same with no clear differentiators. Tom Peters and Robert H. Waterman in their book *In Search of Excellence* identify Frito Lay's (a snack food subsidiary of Pepsi) exceptional customer service as a key differentiator – a service that no doubt cost much more than its rivals.

We might wish to consider what is termed 'best of breed' in a particular area. For example, we may be concerned about our customer service, and rather than comparing ourselves with our competitors, we might look at typical benchmarks across different sectors in the area of customer service and seek to learn how the 'best of breed' actually perform at exceptional levels.

Comparing ourselves against our local (national) competitors is rarely enough in a global market place. We need to consider the competitors who may be on the other side of the world and with whom we may not be competing directly – yet.

Impact of Using Measures

Any overuse of measures as a way of assessing performance can lead to dysfunctional behaviour, e.g. in the NHS (UK) and the HSE (Ireland) actions are often taken to manipulate waiting lists/patients on trolleys. Accountants need to remember **'what you measure is what you get (performance)'**. In other words, if a particular measure achieves significant (over) attention, this can lead to manipulation of measures. (Can you think of a practical example?) Some of these issues are explored in **Exercise 9.1** later in this text.

Another key issue with benchmarking or performance measures is to focus on direction (improvement or disimprovement) rather than the exact measure.

4.4   VALUE CHAIN

Michael Porter, in his book *Competitive Advantage*, describes the value chain as a way of representing how a firm creates value add/profit. The value chain distinguishes primary and support activities. A graphic representation of the value chain (based on Porter):

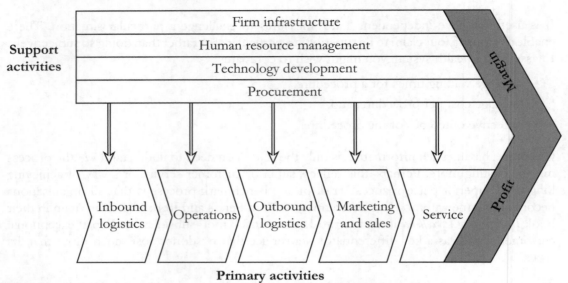

Source: Adapted from Michael E. Porter, *Competitive Advantage: Creating and Sustaining Superior Performance*, New York, The Free Press, 1985.

Figure 4.3: The Value Chain

Key Message of the Value Chain Concept

- We can compare our performance across the value chain analysing how we perform on support and primary activities so as to earn a superior margin.
- Depending on the outcome of the analysis we can determine our response.
- Porter argues that there are two broad ways we can compete. The first is what is termed a differentiator strategy where one provides a superior offering which merits a higher price. The alternative is to be a low-cost operator (what is called a cost leadership strategy) which earns a superior return through higher turnover on a low margin. This is discussed further in Chapter 6.
- Porter warns against getting "stuck in the middle", like Dunnes Stores which is no longer a cost leader (now Lidl/Aldi) nor a differentiator (e.g. 'traditionally' Superquinn/ Sainsbury (UK)).

Exercise 4.10: Value Chain in Ryanair/Aer Lingus

Take the low-cost airline industry and compare this to a traditional national carrier using the value chain model:

Compare Ryanair with Aer Lingus in terms of:

- check in;
- baggage handling;
- boarding; and
- on-flight experience, etc.

Consider the impact on each airline's cost structure and performance.

(See SOLUTIONS at the end of this text.)

Exercise 4.11: Value Chain Application in a Case Study

Apply the value chain to identify strengths and weaknesses in the 'Specky for Eyes' case study (see **Appendix 1**). Using the elements of the value chain, make an assessment of each of the elements (to the extent that the information allows) as a way to identify strengths and weaknesses when compared to Specky for Eyes' competitors.

(See SOLUTIONS at the end of this text.)

4.5   CONCLUSION AND TIPS FOR POSITION AUDIT

From our use of the identified models we can build up a picture of our competencies/strengths and weaknesses. It is important that these differentiators (particularly our strengths) are ones that our customer wants and will pay for. John Kay, an economist, notes that some organisations identify over 40 key differentiators. He notes it is unlikely that these are part of any significant differentiation. We know successful organisations by the key things they are good at.

It is important not to have long lists of strengths or weaknesses. Can the identified issues be grouped logically? If you had two minutes to summarise the key messages what would you focus on or prioritise? It is important that we consider our strengths and weaknesses in the context of our competition.

4.6   SUMMARY – CHAPTER 4

Review the individual models that we have looked at and consider the insights they provide us with in terms of strengths and weaknesses. In particular, consider your skills in the following areas:

- Use an appropriate model to evaluate an organisation's tangible and intangible resources as a basis for assessing an organisation's strengths and weaknesses.
- Apply benchmarking to compare the performance of an organisation against a competitor.
- Apply the value chain to assess the organisation's position.
- Based on appropriate analysis assess an organisation's strengths and weaknesses.

REFERENCES

Tom Peters and Robert H. Waterman Jr., *In Search of Excellence* (Harper, 1982).
Michael Porter, *Competitive Strategy* (The Free Press, 1985).
John Kay, www.johnkay.com (John Kay is a regular contributor to the *Financial Times*).

CHAPTER 5

Corporate Appraisal: SWOT Analysis

Learning Objectives

Having covered the analysis of the environment (opportunities and threats from Chapter 3) and the position audit (strengths and weaknesses in Chapter 4) we now bring these steps together in what is termed a corporate appraisal. The purpose of this chapter is to ensure that you have a clear understanding of the corporate appraisal, or what is termed SWOT (**S**trengths, **W**eaknesses, **O**pportunities and **T**hreats) analysis.

At the end of this chapter you should be able to:

- Undertake a SWOT analysis.
- Assess the size of the strategic gap that needs to be filled.

Pre-reading

Read *Gallagher* Chapter 6, pages 222 onwards. *Gallagher* includes SWOT analysis within the stage of evaluating an organisation's strategic capability.

In terms of our rational model approach to strategy our focus is on the Corporate Appraisal stage as follows:

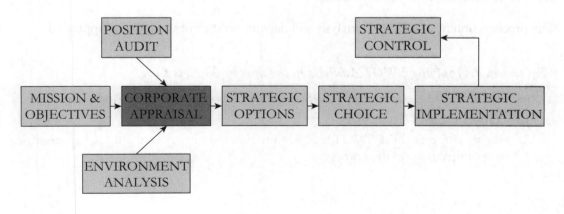

5.1   SWOT ANALYSIS

A diagrammatic representation of SWOT analysis, which highlights the desired actions arising:

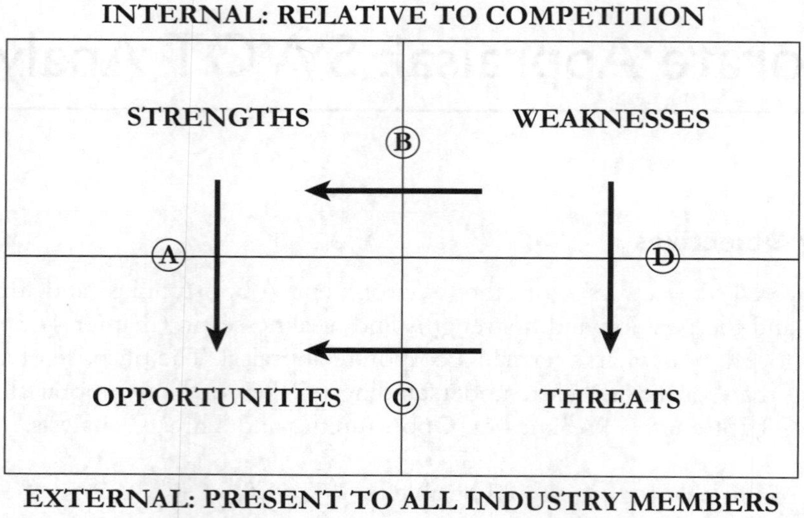

INTERNAL: RELATIVE TO COMPETITION

```
        STRENGTHS         Ⓑ        WEAKNESSES



              ←──────────────

        Ⓐ                              Ⓓ



              ←──────────────

      OPPORTUNITIES    Ⓒ         THREATS
```

EXTERNAL: PRESENT TO ALL INDUSTRY MEMBERS

Figure 5.1: SWOT Analysis

Using SWOT analysis

As a tool, SWOT analysis helps us to bring together our outcomes from the earlier steps. Typically, as illustrated in **Figure 5.1**, our ideal strategies are:

A. Build on our strengths to tackle opportunities
B. Convert weaknesses into strengths
C. Convert threats into opportunities
D. Tackle weaknesses to see off threats

The precise content of a SWOT analysis will depend on the company being appraised.

Exercise 5.1: Applying SWOT Analysis to the Specky for Eyes Case

Using the information contained in the Specky for Eyes case study (see **Appendix 1**):

1. Complete a SWOT analysis.
2. Having completed the SWOT analysis, provide a summary of the three key strategic issues impacting on the company.

Your answer:

STRENGTHS	**WEAKNESSES**
THREATS	**OPPORTUNITIES**

Three key strategic issues:

1.

2.

3.

(See SOLUTIONS at the end of this text.)

Exercise 5.2: Applying SWOT Analysis to Ryanair

Taking Ryanair as an example, identify how they might have dealt with strategic challenges using the SWOT insights:

- Build on strengths to tackle opportunities:

- Convert weaknesses into strengths:

- Convert threats into opportunities:

- Tackle weaknesses to see off threats:

(See SOLUTIONS at the end of this text.)

5.2   GAP ANALYSIS

Gap analysis is a tool which seeks to highlight the future gap that will arise should an organisation continue to pursue the current strategies unchanged as compared to the future objective. This is summarised in the following diagram:

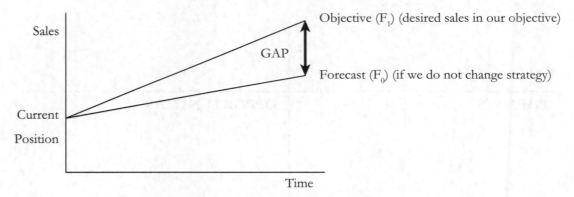

Figure 5.2: Gap Analysis

The F_0 forecast is the projected outcome (in sales or profit) if we continue our existing strategies with no change in strategy. F_1 forecast represents where we want to be in terms of our objective. The identified gap represents the scope of the challenge which our new strategies (to be determined – see Chapter 6) must fill.

Example 5.1: Gap Analysis Practical Example

A company projects the following sales over the next five years based on current strategies and trends:

	Year 1	Year 2	Year 3	Year 4	Year 5
	€´000	€´000	€´000	€´000	€´000
Sales	1,500	1,650	1,750	1,850	1,950
Profit	150	165	175	185	190

Capital Employed	1,000	917	900	1,250	1,200
ROCE	15%	18%	19.4%	14.8%	15.8%
Target ROCE					20%

In this simple example we see the impact of an increase in capital employed (asset replacement) on performance in Year 4 onwards.

In order for the gap to be closed in Year 5, profit will have to increase to €240,000 (or 26%) based on the capital employed of €1.2 million. Is it realistic that through new strategies we could increase our top line (sales) or margin to achieve this?

Limitation/Criticisms of the Gap Analysis Model

It is possible to criticise the use of gap analysis. For example:

- Past trends are not necessarily going to continue (remember those who predicted a 'soft landing' for the Irish economy).
- The difficulty in projecting the future accurately – the future is uncertain.
- The reliability of assumptions underlying our forecast.
- The model does not consider risk.
- It does not consider potential competitor actions, competitor resources or competencies.

5.3   SUMMARY – CHAPTER 5

At this stage you should be familiar with the use and application of SWOT analysis. You were also introduced to the concept of gap analysis.

As with all the models we have mentioned, the 3 Ps apply if you are to develop and hone your skills.

CHAPTER 6

Generating Strategic Options

Learning Objectives

Having assessed (internal) strengths and weaknesses and (external) opportunities and threats, as well as assessing the future gap to be filled, you are now ready to examine the strategic options facing you.

By the end of this chapter you should be able to:

- Differentiate between the alternative approaches to business strategy using Porter's generic strategy model.
- Critically examine the suitability of a particular strategy.
- Distinguish the alternative strategic directions that may be followed.
- Evaluate different strategies in terms of their suitability for a particular company.
- Consider appropriate methods of penetration, market development, product development and diversification options.
- Critically examine the methods of strategic development to achieve growth and suggest appropriate choices which may apply in a particular set of circumstances.

Your FAE Competency Statement includes the following statement:

"Demonstrate an understanding of the key issues which should be addressed in the formulation of strategy to include:
  o competition strategy
  o direction and methods of growth
  o analysis and choice of methods of growth
  o develop strategies relative to its goal bearing in mind the external and social environment in which the organisation operates."

Pre-reading

Read *Gallagher* as follows:

- Chapter 8: Business-level Strategy: this deals with Porter's generic strategies, or in simple terms, asks "how are we going to compete?"
- Chapters 9 and 10 cover the possible strategic directions.
- Chapter 11: Developing Strategic Options covers the alternative growth strategies that can be followed.

Self-assessment

The approach to strategic options is to consider three basic decisions/questions:

1. How are we going to compete to gain competitive advantage? (See **Section 6.2**)
2. What strategic direction are we going to follow? (See **Section 6.3**)
3. How are we going to grow? (See **Section 6.4**)

To support each of these three decisions, we will be referring to:

- Porter's Competitive Theory: the generic strategies
- Strategic Direction, i.e. Ansoff's Product Market Matrix
- The method of growth: in particular the three key approaches to growth.

In terms of our rational model approach to strategy, we are now focusing on strategic options:

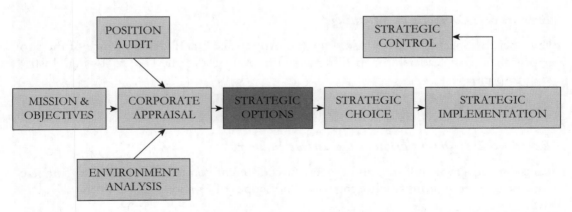

6.1   THE THREE STRATEGIC OPTIONS/QUESTIONS

As noted above there are three key strategic decisions to be addressed:

- How are we going to compete to obtain competitive advantage? (Porter)
- What strategic direction will we follow? (Ansoff)
- What methods of growth will we pursue to achieve the strategic direction?

6.2   COMPETING FOR COMPETITIVE ADVANTAGE

Competitive Advantage

(See also *Gallagher*, Chapter 8.)

Michael Porter in his book *Competitive Advantage* argues that there are two broad ways a company can compete. First, there is cost leadership (e.g. Ryanair), where due to economies and other value chain structures a company can charge lower prices and gain market share. Alternatively, one can differentiate (perhaps through improved service or branding) and justify higher prices. A narrow approach would be to operate on a segmented or niche basis. Visually this is represented as follows:

COMPETITIVE BASIS

Broad	Cost Leadership	Differentiation
SCOPE Narrow	Cost Focus	Differentiation Focus

Figure 6.1: Competitive Advantage

Exercise 6.1: Competitive Advantage

Consider the Specky for Eyes case study (see **Appendix 1**) and identify which of the two approaches (cost leadership and differentiation) you believe they are following? Justify your response.

(See SOLUTIONS at the end of this text.)

Exercise 6.2: Differentiation in the Airline Industry

Consider the airline industry, and suggest how different companies may aim to compete with each other in terms of differing bases and scopes of activity.

(See SOLUTIONS at the end of this text.)

Comment on the Competitive Advantage Model

For a cost leader, ask:

- How are we achieving our low cost base?
- Can competitors imitate our methods?
- Can we defend our cost base?

For differentiators we might ask:

- What are the sources of our competitive differentiation?
- Is it superior products? Can our research and development maintain this lead over time?
- Is it based on marketing and branding? Can our marketing budget support this in the future?
- How are customer tastes and preferences changing regarding the key product (or service) attributes?

6.3   STRATEGIC DIRECTION

Product Market Development (Ansoff)

(See also *Gallagher*, Chapters 9 and 10.)

The Product Market development model was identified by Ansoff in the 1960s. This seeks to identify ways in which we might tackle our market or develop our product (or both). This is represented in the following diagram:

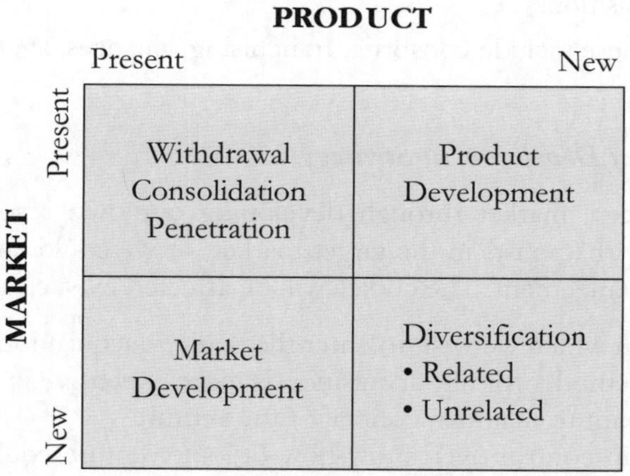

PRODUCT

	Present	New
Present	Withdrawal Consolidation Penetration	Product Development
New	Market Development	Diversification • Related • Unrelated

(**MARKET** on vertical axis)

Figure 6.2: Ansoff Growth Matrix

In determining our choice of approach, we need to consider our competencies and resources when compared to our competitors. For example, adopting a market development strategy assumes we have the experience and resources (compared to our competitors) to tackle a new market. Entering an overseas market can be resource intensive and risky. Similarly, we may wish to develop new products. In this case we might need to consider our previous track record in product development and success at launching products.

Risk is a key issue to be factored into our analysis. Entering new products or markets is a risky strategy compared to staying in our own base.

Exercise 6.3: Apply the Ansoff Matrix to the Specky for Eyes Case Study

For each of the four broad strategies identified by Ansoff, how might Specky for Eyes (see **Appendix 1**) undertake each of the four strategies?

Exercise 6.4: Apply the Ansoff Matrix to your Career as a Chartered Accountant

Can you apply the logic of the Ansoff Matrix to your career as a Chartered Accountant?

(See SOLUTIONS at the end of this text.)

6.4   METHODS OF GROWTH

(See also *Gallagher*, Chapter 11.)

There are three broad methods of growth:

- Internal or organic growth
- Mergers or acquisitions
- Joint venture (these include consortia, franchising, alliances, agencies, etc.)

Example 6.1: Market Development Strategy

We can enter any new market through developing our own resources/competencies, acquiring a company that exists in the target market, or we could enter by way of a joint venture or agency arrangement. The choice will be affected by such factors as:

- The speed with which we wish to enter the market (acquisition is fastest)
- The cost of method (typically acquisition is more expensive in the short term)
- Whether we want to maintain control of the venture
- Desire to retain control over know-how (a joint venture could risk loss of know-how, such as trade secrets)
- Available resources to fund the options (and internal competencies)
- Cultural fit, etc.

In practice, the exploration of alternatives is likely to take some time and may involve periods of high activity.

Each of the identified strategies (penetration, product development, market development, etc.) can be pursued.

Exercise 6.5: Applying Market Development Strategy to the Specky Case

Assuming Specky for Eyes is pursuing a market development strategy, identify how this might be pursued using each of the three identified methods of growth.

SUMMARY – CHAPTER 6

At this stage you should appreciate the strategic options facing the business. We have presented these as involving three steps:

1.   Determine how we wish to compete. Once this is done we are unlikely to change from this, except intermittently.

2.   Determine the strategic choices to be followed; whether to develop new or existing markets or products.

3.   Determine which of the three methods of growth might be used to pursue the identified strategic choice.

You should ensure you have satisfactorily achieved the learning objectives of this chapter before starting the next chapter.

REFERENCES

Igor Ansoff, *Corporate Strategy* (Pan Macmillan, 1965).
Michael Porter, *Competitive Strategy* (The Free Press, 1985).
Johnson, Scholes and Whittington, *Exploring Corporate Strategy*, 8th Ed. (Prentice Hall, 2008).

CHAPTER 7

Strategic Choice

Learning Objectives

Having determined the strategic option, we ultimately have to make a decision or choice. This chapter seeks to highlight the criteria that might guide such decisions.

After studying this chapter you should be able to:

- Recommend appropriate strategic responses to a given set of circumstances, including considering:
  o appropriate criteria to be used in the decision-making process;
  o appropriate decision-making techniques and financial models; and
  o the limitations of the methods used and the information on which this is based.

The FAE Competency Statement requires that you can:

"Advise on preferential strategies bearing in mind suitability, acceptability and feasibility of the identified strategy."

Pre-reading

You should read *Gallagher*, Chapter 12.

Self-assessment

We shall examine the three key criteria on which a decision might be based (per Johnson and Scholes):

- Feasibility
- Acceptability
- Suitability

Study Tip In terms of your studies you will often be asked to make a recommendation based on the information provided. As a guide it is useful to consider:

- What extra information would you like to have before making your decision?
- What sensitivity analysis might be undertaken before making a firm recommendation?
- Are there any overriding non-financial criteria at play?
- Have you considered all aspects of risk?
- Have you got a sufficiently balanced decision or recommendation?

In terms of the rational model, we are focusing on strategic choice as follows:

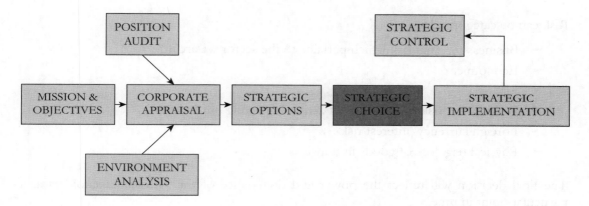

Strategic choice involves considering whether the proposed project or development is acceptable against three identified criteria.

1. Feasibility

- Is the proposed project economically feasible? Does it earn a sufficient financial return? Do we have the resources to undertake it?
- Is it operationally feasible? Will it work within existing or proposed processes/procedures, structures, etc.?
- Is it technically feasible?

There are a range of financial models that might be used such as net present value, return on capital employed, etc. Any assessment should consider the impact of differences in risks.

In your studies of financial management, and management accounting in particular, you will have covered a range of financial management techniques which may be used in any decision-making process. These include:

- Contribution analysis
- Breakeven analysis

- Investment appraisal
- Product profitability analysis
- Customer account profitability analysis
- Sensitivity analysis

2.   Acceptability

Here we focus on the project's acceptability to key stakeholders in terms of risk and return. We highlight key stakeholders, typically shareholders, but there may be other 'key players' who will be central to the project's success.

Risk can be categorised as:

- Business (i.e. that risk which pertains to the sector we are in)
- Economic
- Financial
- Political (i.e. risk of government action impacting our business)
- Foreign currency/interest risk
- Physical (e.g. loss of goods in transit)

The final decision will reflect the power and dominance of the various stakeholders at a particular point in time.

3.   Suitability

Does the proposed strategy:

- Exploit opportunities? (from our environmental analysis — see Chapter 3)
- Play to our strengths?
- Address identified weaknesses? (See Chapter 4)
- Mitigate threats?
- Close the identified gap?
- Achieve our strategic intent?

In practical terms, such analysis and decision-making is rarely easy. We are regularly facing incomplete information and uncertainty to add to what is likely to be a complex problem.

> ### Example 7.1: Coca-Cola: An Example of a Failed Decision
>
> In the 1980s, The Coca-Cola Company decided to change its flavour to compete with Pepsi. This followed a successful challenge from Pepsi ('the Pepsi challenge') where customers were given a blind tastes test between Coca-Cola and Pepsi. Market research,

taster tests and so forth elicited favourable responses to the change so, after this evaluation exercise, the new formulation was introduced. However, a small group of consumers vociferously opposed the change, and this opposition spread suddenly and rapidly like an epidemic, forcing The Coca-Cola Company to re-introduce the old formula.

Apparently some consumers perceived Coca-Cola to symbolise 'American values', and changing the formula appeared to be an insult to them. Despite the absence of the Internet, this reaction gained momentum.

Other consumers, who had initially favoured the product, turned against it for reasons that could not be predicted by market researchers. This exemplifies:

- The limitations of planning.
- The seemingly random behaviour of the environment (as it became fashionable *not* to drink the new formula).
- The way in which small causes (a few disaffected Coca-Cola drinkers) can generate major consequences.
- The limitations of organisational gathering of information and strategic evaluation.

SUMMARY – CHAPTER 7

At this stage you should be familiar with the three criteria which should apply to your decision:

- **F**easibility   –   **F**
- **A**cceptability   –   **A**
- **S**uitability   –   **S**

As we have noted in earlier chapters, you should practise using these criteria to assess situations in your personal life and the business/organisation in which you work.

REFERENCES

Johnson, Scholes and Whittington, *Exploring Corporate Strategy*, 8th Edition (Prentice Hall, 2008).

CHAPTER 8

Strategy Implementation: Preparing a Detailed Business Plan

Learning Objectives

The purpose of this chapter is to ensure that you have a clear understanding of how to approach the implementation of strategy. In particular, we will look at how to develop the contents of a business plan. In practical terms, having a near perfect plan or strategy is not enough – it is in the execution of the strategy that problems often arise.

At the end of this chapter you should be able to:

- Outline/draft a plan to implement the agreed strategy;
- Outline a functional plan based on an agreed strategy and ensure that this is aligned to the business strategy;
- Identify issues in implementing the plan and how these might be managed.

The FAE competency statement requires that you can:

- "Draft a business plan. Critique a business plan."
- "Assess the implications of these strategies for the organisation…"
- "Advise on appropriate methods to communicate an entity's strategy, outline the impact of the strategy on other business functions, highlight resource issues in the strategy selection and implementation process.
- Outline the impact of strategy on organisational structures, cultures, and management styles."

Pre-reading

Read *Gallagher*, Chapter 13.

Self-assessment

Before proceeding, think about your awareness of the issues to be addressed in strategy implementation. For example:

- What are the issues that will need to be considered in planning for strategy implementation? (See **Section 8.1**)

- What would the typical contents of a business plan be? (See **Section 8.2**)
- Can you prepare or draft a business plan or elements of a plan? (See **Section 8.3**)
- What are the possible impediments to the successful implementation of a strategy and how might these be handled? (See **Section 8.4**)

In terms of the rational model approach to strategy, we are focusing on the implementation phase:

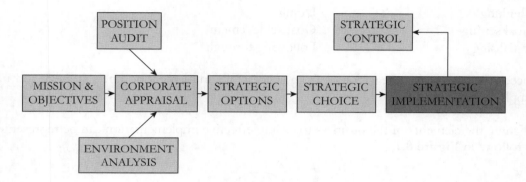

8.1   BUSINESS PLANNING

Why Have a Plan?

Any business plan must have a strategic basis. The business plan's purpose is to convert the strategy into a detailed plan to guide, direct and motivate staff. There is no purpose in strategic planning if it does not lead to implementation. By writing and developing a plan we can hopefully make our errors on paper and avoid mistakes in the market place.

A business plan will support management in running the business. It acts as a framework within which detailed projections and budgets can be prepared. In due course the plan will enable management to monitor progress.

Plans support communication to the whole organisation. Not everyone will need to see the full plan, but it needs to be in sufficient detail so that each individual staff member knows what it means for them and what is expected from them. A plan may also be used to seek finance from a bank or additional resources. The nature, form and detail will depend on the audience and the use to which it will be put.

Exercise 8.1: Practical Question – A Business Plan to Support a Finance Application

You are a bank manager who has been approached by a newly-formed business seeking funds to support the development of a product and new markets. Identify the areas which you believe should be covered and why.

(See SOLUTIONS at the end of this text.)

Implementation of any plan is a critical phase – it is converting the ideas into action in order to generate results. It will require significant management attention. This is where things often fail. The differences between strategy formulation and implementation can be seen in the words used to describe both:

From: **Strategy Formulation**	To: **Strategy Implementation**
Analysis	Execution
Thinking	Doing
Goal setting	Goal achievement
Initialising	Following through

Success in terms of strategy comes from successfully implementing one's strategy and not simply having a strategy!

Aligning the elements of the business to ensure effective implementation can be represented as follows in **Figure 8.1**.

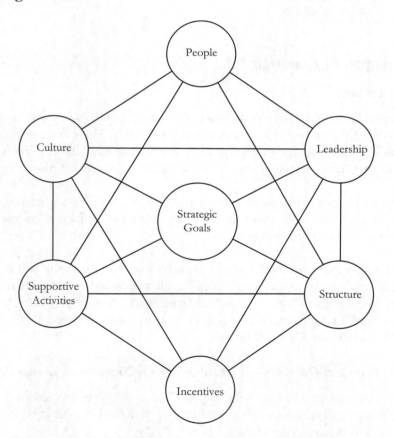

Figure 8.1: Alignment for Implementation

People and Incentives We need to ensure that we have the appropriate people with the necessary skills and experience to implement the necessary strategy. Incentives need to be adjusted and developed so that staff are motivated to implement the proposed strategy.

Supportive Activities Any system is made up of interrelated parts, and it is crucial that these various subsystems work together to support the overall strategy. (See Southwest Airlines example below in **Figure 8.2**.)

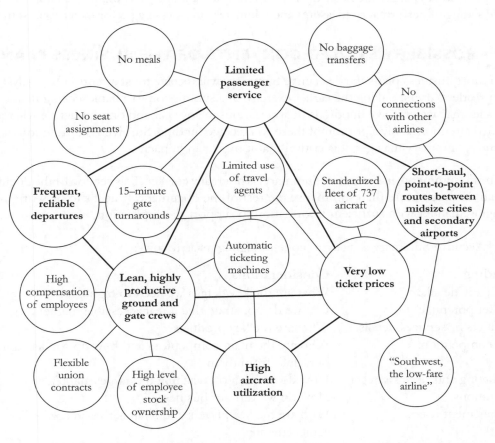

Source: Michael E. Porter, "What Is Strategy?" *Harvard Business Review*, November–December 1996, 73. Reproduced with permission.

Figure 8.2: Southwest Airlines Activity System

Organisational Structure The implementation of any new plan may need changes to be made to the existing structure; hence the phrase 'structure follows strategy'.

Culture and Leadership Culture refers to the organisation's values, traditions and operating style. A strong culture aligned to strategy can assist the implementation of that strategy. However, a strong culture can be hard to change. For example, building a new customer service culture where a 'bureaucratic' culture previously existed is likely to be a slow, arduous process. It is vital that the CEO and top management model the culture and behaviour desired. Full engagement with staff is needed, with appropriate rewards and incentives, for the adoption of the appropriate behaviour/culture.

For each of the identified areas (people and incentives, support activities, organisational structure, and culture and leadership), we need to be clear on whether they are all suitable and aligned to our strategy or what changes are needed. As Chartered Accountants, you will play an important role in the setting of performance measures and, ultimately, in assessing performance against these.

8.2   POSSIBLE DETAILED CONTENTS OF THE BUSINESS PLAN

With most business plans the Executive Summary will receive most attention by analysts and other readers/users. Taking the earlier exercise of a submission to a bank seeking finance, the financier may well receive hundreds of applications in any year and only a fraction will receive detailed attention. Only a portion of these will receive funding. So, given the attention that the executive summary may get, it is critical that it makes an impact.

The term 'summary' (in Executive Summary) is not really correct. This section of the document should do much more than summarise the rest of the document. It needs to be written in an engaging manner with sufficient information to support the application.

The Executive Summary is likely to contain highlights as follows:

Heading	Considerations
Company details:	What are the key details we need to highlight?
Market potential:	Can we demonstrate that a real accessible market exists?
Products or services details:	What are the key products?
The competition:	Who are the main competitors and how do we distinguish ourselves from them?
Marketing and sales strategy:	How do we plan on reaching our target market?
Operations:	How do we run our business?
Management team:	Who are the key players and what is their record of achievement?
Future strategies:	Where do we want to be in five years?
Financials:	What are the key financial targets and returns?

Some Pointers

- Given the nature of the Executive Summary, it is likely to be the last item drafted when the rest of the plan has been written in full. In preparing the summary, it is necessary to step back and ask what the intended readers' needs are (e.g. the lender). You may benefit from the input of others who could assist in answering such issues as: What information is missing? What was unsatisfactory? What else would they wish to see?

- A table of contents often follows the Executive Summary. This is designed to enable the reader to navigate to key areas of interest or to quickly dip into matters of interest in more detail. The order of items in the table of contents should reflect their relative importance. The financial details are likely to follow the key issues of marketing and management – remember finance is a means to an end and not an end in itself.

- Remember: the layout of the document creates an impression of the individuals who run the organisation. It should communicate that they are serious about this proposal and their approach to the document should reflect this.

Exercise 8.2: Contents of the Business Plan

Look at each of the identified headings in the Executive Summary note above. For each of the headings list the possible contents in each section in the main body of the report.

(See SOLUTIONS at the end of this text.)

Other Considerations

How long should the business plan be?

The length and detail of any business plan/finance plan will need to reflect:

- The size and nature of the organisation
- The amount of money being sought (assuming this is the reason it is being prepared)
- The type of finance being sought
- The specific issues to be addressed.

A 'standard' application for loan finance to a venture capitalist is likely to be significantly longer than an application for major funding from a bank. Think of the reader's preferences and ask them if you do not know.

Presenting the Plan

Most plans will be written and it is worth thinking about how layout and presentation can be used to create an appropriate impression. The use of colour, diagrams and photos can help strengthen the document. Tables are a useful way to summarise large volumes of data and, as far as possible, detail should be put in appendices.

A PowerPoint or similar presentation format is normally also required to support the printed document.

8.3 DRAFTING DEPARTMENTAL AND FUNCTIONAL PLANS

Any plan for a business will by definition be 'high level' – it cannot go into the level of detail that will be necessary at a departmental or functional level. Having created a business plan and identified the key areas to be addressed, it will be necessary to determine the implications in terms of details for each of the separate sections, departments and functions. On a practical basis it is necessary to spell out the detail in terms of:

- Planned changes in work practices or operations
- Timing of planned changes
- Key performance indicators
- Monitoring processes.

At a personal level, you will have agreed a set of goals for your job based on your appraisal. If these are to be effective, these goals should be aligned to the department's goals and, in turn, to the organisation's goals. Too often the identified goals are not SMART (or SMARTER) and progress against these is not monitored.

A useful way of remembering this is:

Exercise 8.3: Functional Plans

You are a product manager in a fast-moving consumer products company. Top management strategy has indicated a desire to increase your revenues by 4% in the coming year. As manager for your section, you have been asked to draft the plan. You have identified a range of cheaper product offerings from a supplier in the Far East which may be preferred by customers in these tight economic times.

Requirement: List some of the actions you might take to develop your plan.

(See SOLUTIONS at the end of this text.)

Functional Strategies in More Detail

For each of the functional areas objectives will need to be set which are aligned to the overall strategy. The nature of the functional strategy will vary and depend on the overall strategy. You should consider how the proposed strategy will impact on each functional area (or what key areas need to change in each function if the strategy is to be delivered). A high-level review of some of the key aspects of the functional strategies follows.

Finance Strategy

The financing strategy must balance:

- Funding strategies, which must consider the business and financing needs over time in line with the strategy, as well as related risks.
- Managing the value drivers of the business – by adopting a *shareholder value analysis* perspective, one can increase shareholder wealth through:
  - o   Growing the sales ahead of inflation
  - o   Increasing margin or cutting costs
  - o   Reducing surplus assets or working capital
  - o   Minimising tax liability
  - o   Minimising cost of capital
- Managing financial *expectations* of stakeholders regarding risk, return, etc.

Marketing Strategy (High-level issues only)

The marketing strategy will need to cover:

- Building and maintaining brands: many leading FMCG organisations such as Unilever focus on leading brands only.
- Managing resources required to build and develop the product portfolio and allocate resources between them.
- The radical impact of e-business models and the Internet on marketing strategies.

HR Strategy

HR (Human Resources) strategy will typically focus on:

- Managing people as a resource:
  - o   setting appropriate performance measures to achieve our strategy; and
  - o   developing and maintaining personal competences in line with the organisation developments and strategies.
- Recognising the *cultural/political* context and the need to have appropriate management and styles.
- Adopting *modern* organisation approaches such as flatter hierarchies and teamwork, out-sourcing as needed.

Communicating the Plan

Most of the issues regarding the formal communication of the plan have been outlined above. Some additional issues to consider include:

- What message(s) is/are to be conveyed?
- How might this message be worded/constructed? In written or oral form, for example.

- What means of transmission should be used?

- What action/thoughts/feelings do we want the audience to have when they hear the message?

- What messages have gone before? What is the 'normal' way that such messages are communicated?

- Is the message aligned to our values and mission?

- Where is the message to be communicated?

- Are there audio visual or other technological requirements?

For Written Communications

Consider:

- What does the reader/audience know already?

- Are there a number of separate discrete groups being targeted?

- How much time does the reader have?

- What are the key areas of interest for the reader?

- What are their preferences in terms of length and language?

- What are the key messages, and how can a case be made?

- How much familiarity does the reader have with the issue at hand?

- What are the financial considerations, and how can these be best expressed (tables are generally preferred)?

- Would you be willing to pay for what you write?

- What are the key issues or priorities? Are you comfortable with the accuracy of your report? Are there any key assumptions? Is your work objective?

- In real life situations a report is likely to go through a series of drafts. In an examination setting you are unlikely to have time to revise.

- Your writing style should seek to meet the needs and expectations of the reader. Jargon and slang should be avoided.

- Are you clear on your overall objective? This will vary if you are writing as a dispassionate consultant or an insider, or indeed for a third party.

- Is a balanced impartial perspective needed where a full discussion of the pros and cons of a particular plan are needed? A useful question to ask might be "what do I want the reader to say, think and feel having read this document?"

- Have you clarified any resource issues? You should consider the resources available to you before you begin writing:
  - Any budget available
  - Time allowed
  - Research reports available
  - Equipment
  - Colleagues available to consult with

- Have you checked that:
  - o   The terms of reference have been adhered to?
  - o   The reader's needs have been met?
  - o   Your objectives have been met?

8.4   IMPLEMENTING THE PLAN

Implementation issues include:

- Changes in organisation structure
- Change management
- Performance measures (covered in Chapter 9)

(Read *Gallagher*, Chapters 13 and 14.)

Organisation Structure

Organisation structure is covered in *Gallagher*, Chapter 7. One key message is that *organisation structure should follow from the strategy*. Another way of saying this is that a poor organisation structure can impede the implementation of strategy. It is critical that any change(s) in structure and processes is/are thought through, including:

- Communication of the changes
- Top management support
- Adjustments to the reward systems or bonuses
- Training and staff development
- Managing the risks involved
- Change management processes (see below) and so on.

Change Management

Change management is covered elsewhere in your materials and in the *Gallagher* text. Implementing any strategy involves change and the lessons and tools of change management should be adopted. We might start by recalling some key reasons for successful change.

The key reasons for success are:

- **A clear shared vision** For staff to be able to make the transition to the new process, systems or plans, a clear picture is needed of where they are going. Such a 'shared vision' can act as a motivator for all.
- **Effective sponsorship** Top management (and front line managers) need to show active and visible support for the change and ensure that this remains a priority. Change agents and external consultants can be used to support the change.
- **Effective communication** It is important that the reason for the change is explained and justified. In particular the question "what does this change mean for me?" needs to be answered for each affected staff member. The communications need to be honest

and targeted at the relevant groups at the right time. Resistance to change needs to be anticipated and managed accordingly.

- **Proper project planning** Any change process can be viewed as a project in its own right and it needs to be managed accordingly. The project team needs to have the appropriate spread of skills, experience and authority.

- **Sufficient resources are allocated** Pushing through a programme of change in a situation where staff are already stretched with their 'day job' is a recipe for failure. Staff need to have the resources and time to manage and progress the change.

Exercise 8.4: Failed Project Implementation

You are the Financial Controller in Infosys, a vendor of laptops and other executive gadgets. Sales take place through a sales team who are paid on a commission basis. Up to now the sales people have maintained their own sales and other records on their customers. The records were held in a database, but access was limited to each individual sales staff member only. Each salesperson had their own group of customers which they serviced. Each salesperson has viewed the customers as his/her "own".

Up to recent times this arrangement worked reasonably well with most salesmen managing to meet or exceed targets in the buoyant economy. However, the recent economic downturn has resulted in increased cost cutting by competitors and competition via the Internet. Customers have indicated that besides price they are attracted to competitors who are able to service their needs; in the words of one customer: "I cannot wait until your salesmen get around to responding to my needs". The fragmented nature of the database was thus adding to these difficulties.

Consequently, as Financial Controller, you have worked with your IT department to roll out a new company-wide customer relationship management system. This is based on the company's intranet. This would enable all sales staff to see all customer details and thus reduce the risk of lost orders.

The layout and design of the system involved user input in the design of the screens and reports. Unfortunately, due to a shortage of resources and pressure to make progress, the system was introduced in a hurry and the planned user validation and acceptance testing did not take place. Indeed, some last-minute changes were made to make the system perform faster but at the expense of the planned user-friendly features. The roll-out of the new system took place during the summer months and consequently many staff missed training, as they were on leave.

A number of 'bugs' arose in the new system and, though these have now been addressed, this added to a level of distrust in the new system amongst sales staff. Sales staff have continued to be rewarded on an individual basis.

It is now seven months since the implementation took place. You note that the sales team have continued to maintain and use their own records as before and the new system is effectively ignored.

You are required to:

- Identify the reasons for the failed implementation
- Suggest a specific action which might be taken to address each issue

(See SOLUTIONS at the end of this text.)

In crafting any plan, you should always consider:

- **Keep it simple** A complex plan is likely to confuse and frustrate subordinates.
- **Involve** those who will execute the plan in the development of the plan – this should engender greater 'buy-in'.
- **'Eating an elephant'** Any plan should be broken into manageable chunks so staff have a sense of it being doable and progress.
- **Be clear** about roles and responsibilities – who will be answerable for each part? Make sure staff sign up to this.
- **Keep it flexible** Murphy's (or Sod's) Law will always apply, so we need to be able to adapt and respond to changing circumstances and not be too rigid.
- **Performance metrics** Have we got clear performance metrics of what is expected and by when?
- **Resources** Have the necessary resources been put in place?

SUMMARY – CHAPTER 8

At this stage, you should be able to:

- Outline the contents of a business plan;
- Prepare a business plan or part of one; and
- Consider aspects of implementation including organisation, structural changes and change management.

You should ensure you have satisfactorily achieved the learning objectives of this section/ chapter before starting the next chapter.

REFERENCES

Abrams, Barrow, *The Successful Business Plan* (The Planning Shop, 2005).
Blackwell, *How to Prepare a Business Plan*, 4th Edition (Kogan Page, 2004).
Barrow, Barrow, Brown, *The Business Plan Workbook*, 6th Edition (Kogan Page, 2008).
Brian O'Kane, *Starting a Business in Ireland*, 4th Edition (Oak Tree Press, 2004).
Johnson, Scholes and Whitington, *Exploring Corporate Strategy*, 8th Edition (Prentice Hall, 2008).
Richard Luecke, *Strategy: Create and Implement the Best Strategy for Business*, Harvard Business Essentials (Harvard Business Press, 2005).
Lyons, Prone, *This Business of Writing* (ICAI, 2006) is a useful guide to writing styles.

CHAPTER 9

Strategic Control

Learning Objectives

The purpose of this chapter is to ensure that you have a clear understanding of the ways in which the progress of the business plan may be monitored and controlled.

Having covered this material you should be able to:

- Identify appropriate measures to monitor the progress of any plan and strategic project;
- Select appropriate measures, bearing in mind the limitations of the various methods;
- Appreciate the issues and processes involved in project management.

Your Competency Statement requires that you can:

- "Advise on the implementation and monitoring of strategies."

Pre-reading

Read *Gallagher,* Chapter 13.

Self-assessment

Before proceeding, reflect on your awareness of performance measures and how they are used to assess progress. You might also think about how project management tools can assist this process.

In terms of our rational model of strategy our focus is on the strategic control phase:

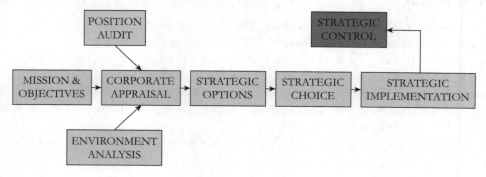

9.1 PERFORMANCE MEASURES

As Chartered Accountants you will know from your studies of traditional accounting measures of performance such as profit, return on capital employed, earnings per share, net present value, cash flow, etc. Each of these measures seeks to assess how the business has done in the past and to provide guidance on what needs to be done in the future.

Before looking at traditional and modern approaches to performance measurement, it is worth reminding ourselves of the traditional approach to control. This reflected a 'theory X' view of the worker and hence it:

- focused on rules and procedures, and supervision
- relied on penalties and sanctions to ensure compliance
- relied on budgets and variances; and
- centralised decision-making

Such an approach was reflected in the management and cost accounting systems. It is recognised that there were consequential problems in traditional accounting techniques which typically compare with modern systems as follows:

Traditional Performance System	Modern Performance System
Does not address what drives cost	ABC approach
Ignores cost structures	Marginal costing
Short-term perspectives	Longer-term perspective
Financial measures only	Balanced Scorecard
Internal focus	External measures/benchmarks

In your management accounting studies you will have seen that responsibility accounting uses a number of responsibility centres to manage performance and ensure goals are achieved. These are:

- **Cost centres** Here we manage the cost of operating a particular function, cost per unit and perhaps ratios or measures such as activity or production, down time, etc.
- **Profit centres** Here the manager is considered to have control over the revenue stream and the costs and thus is managed by assessing performance of the profit centre against target.
- **Investment centres** Here the manager is considered to have control over the costs, revenues and investment. At this level managers are evaluated using such measures as ROCE or residual income.

Non-Financial Measures of Performance

You will appreciate that financial measures alone are increasingly seen as insufficient. Other measures of performance are being included as a means of assessing how we are doing. Examples of non-financial measures are given below:

- **Service quality:**
  - Number of complaints/waiting time/repeats/on-time delivery

- **Production:**
  - o Set up time/days stock on hand/mats yield/rework level/lead times/output per employee
- **Marketing:**
  - o Market share/sales growth/customer visits per salesman/sales volume vs forecast, etc.
- **Personnel:**
  - o Number of complaints recorded
  - o Staff turnover
  - o Absenteeism
  - o Accidents or sickness days
  - o Training time per employee

Of course, having additional measures of a non-financial nature is not enough. There is a risk of management overload if managers are receiving too many numbers. (Think of an airline pilot and his/her need to monitor the performance of the plane.)

The key questions we must address are:

- What are the key strategic objectives we have set for ourselves over the next year/five years?
- What key performance indicators can be used to measure progress? In simple terms "what does 'good' look like?" or, if you like, what key measures, if achieved, will pay significant dividends?

Other important considerations are:

- What are the underlying *assumptions* of the measure? For example, a high number of students achieving first class honours may appear to be a good result for the university – if we assume that academic and quality controls are strong.

- How *many* measures to have? Rather than having multiple measures, it is preferable to have a small number, even if these are not complete. This allows us to assess progress and direction.

- How *frequently* to measure? Measuring and assessing how your pension is doing on a day-to-day basis is unlikely to be appropriate. The frequency of the measuring will depend on what is being measured and the cycles in which it operates.

- How will the measure impact on *behaviour*? Remember WYMIWYG (what you measure is what you get.) Consider the impact of assigning marks in your FAE to attendance at the FAE education programme – physical attendance is not necessarily a good indicator of learning.

- Are the measures *balanced*? A Balanced Scorecard is suggested. This recognises in a balanced way the need for:
  - o **Financial measures** aligned to our strategy
  - o **Customer measures** which are seeking to support the strategy and which are important to our customer

o **Learning measures** focusing on areas we need to innovate if we are to succeed in the long term
o **Process measures** to ensure we are efficient in our internal processes.

The KPIs should be selected to support the overall objectives in a balanced way:

- Do the measures focus too much on the short term?
- Can they be manipulated? How might we compensate for this?
- How do the measures link to rewards and risk?

Exercise 9.1: Using KPIs and implementing the Balanced Scorecard

Background/Outline You are a recently qualified Chartered Accountant working in CA Consult, a consulting firm. Your boss advises you that CA Consult has recently secured an assignment to assist the Authority for Higher Education (AHE) in its allocation of funding to a number of universities across the island of Ireland.

A schedule of data on the performance of the four universities which are eligible for funding is given in **Appendix 1**. The AHE has a sum of €20 million which it wishes to allocate to the universities. It has yet to decide whether a single grant should be paid to one university alone or whether it should be divided amongst them. All universities in the country were asked to make submissions and, following a review by the AHE, a short list of universities has been drawn up. Each has been asked to submit specific data on their financial and other performances. This data has been compiled by the AHE and included in **Appendix 1**. This is not all the potential information available and you should consider what else might be of assistance to you.

Your boss states: "We will be meeting with Mr Frank Murphy of the AHE next Monday. In advance of this I want you to prepare a briefing note addressing the issues as you see them. We can discuss this on Friday and clarify our thinking in advance of the meeting."

You are required to prepare the briefing paper for your superior for the Friday meeting.

Appendix 1

Analysis of information available from four universities

	Notes	Belfast University	Eastern Dublin University	Southern University	Western University
Surplus/(Deficit)					
2011	1	€1.2m	€0.2m	€0.1m	€(0.2m)
2010		€0.9m	€.5m	€1.3m	€(0.9m)

Grants received	2	€15m	€15m	€3m	€1m
Fee income	3	€45m	€66m	€51m	€40m
Non-fee income	3	€3m	€13m	€2m	0
Number of students					
Undergraduate	5	7,500	12,450	9,700	5,400
Postgraduate	5	1,250	2,457	1,950	750
Non-national students as % of total		2%	7%	3%	15%
Lecturing staff	6	202	410	220	102
Support staff	6	420	690	450	78
Average entry criteria	7	500	510	460	420
Actual average points achieved	8	480	520	455	480
% of students gaining a:					
1st degree	9	8%	5%	4%	12%
2.1 honours		22%	22%	15%	28%
2.2 honours		30%	28%	41%	30%
Dropout rate	10	5%	8%	4%	2%
% of graduates unemployed	11	6%	3%	8%	3%
Lecturer average contact hours	12	600	690	750	800
Average number of published articles by lecturer	13	4	6	3	2
Average number of publications by college	14	54	32	12	41
Average lecturer salary	15	€55,000	€75,000	€80,000	€68,000
Average support staff salary	15	€29,000	€37,000	€35,000	€32,000

Notes:

1. Universities are expected to manage their finances so as to cover their costs. In recent years the abolition of student fees in the southern universities has led to a deteriorating position in these institutions.
2. Grants are made available from central exchequer to support the development of the universities. The allocation of funds has historically been made, based on two criteria:
   (a) political pressure applied by local politicians; and
   (b) strategic objectives set by the Government.
3. In lieu of student fees, a grant is made by the Government in the case of the three southern universities.
4. Non-grant income represents income generated by the college from research undertaken, accommodation fees charged, conference fees, and so on.
5. Student numbers are for the 2010–2011 academic year and have been reasonably stable over the last few years.
6. Staff numbers are based on full-time equivalents, i.e. where staff work part-time the number has been adjusted proportionately.

7. Entry criteria onto undergraduate programmes are based on performance in the final school examination. This is scored out of a maximum 600 points. The entry criteria are set based on the needs of individual programmes as well as anticipated demand and are set prior to applications being made. This has been averaged across all faculties.

8. Actual average points achieved reflects the actual average number of points scored by individuals in their examination. In some cases, the demand has not met the anticipated criteria under 7.

9. All results are based on the most recent examinations, including repeat sessions where applicable.

10. Dropout rates represent the number of first year students who have discontinued their studies.

11. The percentage of unemployed is calculated based on an online survey of graduates completed approximately six months after graduation.

12. The number of contact hours is affected by several criteria, including class sizes, the amount of research undertaken and whether one is lecturing to postgraduate students.

13. Numbers are based on publications in academically recognised publications.

14. Books published by staff in each university in 2010–2011.

15. Average salary depends on the length of tenure of staff and their grading. A scale system is in place.

Requirement:

- Identify three key questions you would wish to ask your client at your first meeting.
- List possible other useful information you would like to get to assist your work.
- Undertake an analysis of the data provided.
- On the basis that a Balanced Scorecard is to be developed to assess the colleges, outline the possible practical steps that might be taken to roll this out.

(See SOLUTIONS at the end of this text.)

9.2 PROJECT MANAGEMENT

Many projects are strategic and are critical to our future success. As such, they need particular attention and active management. One way of looking at the implementation and control of a business strategy or plan is to think of it as a major area of change, as a *project*, and to manage it accordingly. This final section of the workbook reviews some of the concepts and ideas of project management which can assist you in the implementation and control phases.

In managing any project or plan it is worth reminding ourselves of the four key dimensions of a project:

- Scope
- Quality
- Budget
- Timescale

In managing any project or assignment it is possible to trade these dimensions off against one another:

- For example, it is normally possible to achieve our result faster by increasing our budget (up to a point) or by reducing quality checks, etc.
- Take a job or project you are familiar with, say an audit. Consider how the four identified dimensions were managed and how pressure from your client (or boss) impacted on the progress of the assignment.

Why Projects Succeed

The top three reasons that lead to project success are:

- user involvement;
- executive management support; and
- a clear statement of requirements.

Why Projects Go Wrong

Managing projects often involves recognising that things will turn out differently to how they were planned. The key point is that you actively manage the outcome and plan for the next steps. Typical reasons why projects fail can be categorised into:

- **Over-optimism** Perhaps we failed to "read the signs" or were persuaded to be more optimistic to ensure the project was approved.
- **Changing specification** Commonly through poor project management the scope is allowed to grow – often for apparently valid reasons, without a corresponding increase in resources or reflection on the implications. The HSE PPARS HR and Payroll IT project is an example of scope creep.
- **Poor project management**.
- **Lack of support**, particularly from top management.

Project Life Cycle

Each project can be considered to have four phases in its lifecycle:

1. **Concept** – the scope of the project is agreed and defined.
2. **Development phase** – a more detailed working system is developed.
3. **Implementation phase** – the delivery of the project.
4. **Close-out** – work is completed and accepted by the client/user.

A project must successfully pass through each phase in order to progress to the next. Management review can take place at any point which can allow for termination at each stage (see your IT notes for more on this).

Overview of Project Management Tools

To assist the project manager, typical tools that are used to manage time and resources are:

- **Gantt Charts**:
  - o Bar line chart
  - o The various activities can be linked to show knock-on effects
- **Critical Path Analysis**:
  - o Maps the activities and the relationship between them. This requires that we have identified all activities and the sequencing of them. Activities are represented by arrows which link a series of points or nodes. We need to know how long each activity will take.
  - o The sequence of activities and how long they are going to take. A project network technique is used to predict total project duration.
  - o Critical path or minimum amount of time. A critical path for a project is the series of activities that determines the ***earliest time*** by which the project can be completed. It is the ***longest path*** through the network diagram and has the least amount of slack time.
  - o Tools such as Microsoft 'Project' can help to automate this.

9.3 STAYING ON COURSE

Many strategies fail because they are not executed well. Assuming we have developed a detailed action plan to implement each goal, we can monitor progress and determine if problems are occurring. The following simple model might be used to find and implement problems (from Richard Luecke, *Strategy: Create and Implement the Best Strategy for your Business* (Harvard Business Press, 2005, p.97).

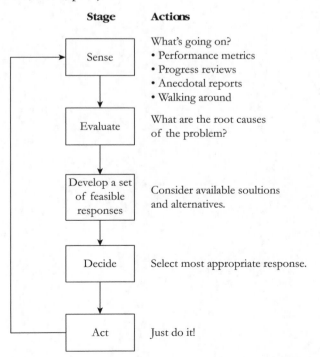

Typically, problems of execution centre on the following points:

- Do staff have appropriate resources?
- Do staff have appropriate skills?
- Are the objectives/goals *still* realistic?
- Has our situation changed significantly?
- Are there communication problems:
    o Does everyone know the nature and purpose of the strategy and why it's being done, as well as the consequences of failure or doing nothing?
    o Can everyone assess progress? Is progress linked to reward?

SUMMARY – CHAPTER 9

At this stage, you should have a clear grasp of how KPIs are used to assess, monitor and control progress of our strategy implementation.

REFERENCES

Kathy Schwalbe, *Information Technology Project Management* (Thomson Learning, 2005) was used as a basis for writing the sections on project management.
Richard Luecke, *Strategy: Create and Implement the Best Strategy for Your Business,* Harvard Business Essentials (Harvard Business Press, 2005).

Case Study: "Specky for Eyes"

John Specky founded Specky for Eyes Limited, an opticians shop based in Dublin, in 1958. The original store was on Abbey Street, where the numbers of on-street shoppers declined over the years until the arrival of the new Dublin tramway system (the Luas) which passes in front of the store. Glasses frames were sourced originally from the UK, though a wider range of suppliers have been found in Europe and the Far East.

Over the years, the company developed a number of additional glasses stores based on main streets in the Dublin area. There are now four stores in the chain, some of which are in leased premises while others (including the original Abbey Street property) are owned.

In the initial 40 years of its existence, the company established a good reputation for service and reliability amongst a loyal customer base. Customers were attracted by its traditional and reasonably priced selection of glasses, or 'spectacles' as the company referred to them. Normally, customers obtained a prescription for their glasses and then went to the store to purchase a pair of frames. The store took a number of days to source the lens and the customer would come in after a week for a final fitting. The company has traditionally shunned any formal marketing (though the new Chief Operating Officer (COO) has plans in this area – this is discussed in more detail later on). This was justified by the belief that if you have a good product, customers will come. Newer competitor chains of opticians have adopted an aggressive marketing campaign to try to penetrate the market and create brand awareness.

Over the last 10 years, Specky for Eyes has faced increasing competition from a range of new glasses stores. These offer one-stop-shop arrangements with opticians on site and a wider range of 'designer' frames. These stores are located in new suburban shopping centres with convenient opening hours and fast turnaround times. Many customers can have their new glasses fitted out within a few hours, or typically within 48 hours.

John Specky continues to run the business as it always has been run. He maintains a high level of control over each store, receiving weekly cash sales reports, with all expenses being sent to him for sign-off. In this way, he retains tight control over expenses, though in practice, the volume of paper work and double checking is very time-consuming. He is rapidly approaching his retirement and a new COO was recently recruited. John remains heavily involved in the day-to-day operations of the business.

The glasses industry has undergone rapid technological change in recent years with newer materials and designs being adopted. Newer technologies enable the rapid assessment of needs, and this has resulted in improved customer service. Increased economic prosperity has increased disposable income, and many customers, instead of having only one pair of glasses, may have a number of pairs, including prescription sunglasses.

Specky for Eyes' response to the changes in technology and customer tastes has been a conservative one. "We have operated in a consistent way for the last 50 years and we have a loyal customer base," was John Specky's response when challenged. "My staff are loyal – many have been with me for nearly 40 years – and we have a well-established way of doing business," he added. There are limited prospects for progression in the chain. Nonetheless, many of Mr Specky's staff remain very loyal to him. "He gave us jobs when there were not many," one staff member commented. Job descriptions and working conditions were all managed centrally by Mr Specky. Once a new staff member settled into the role, the job provided a high level of predictability and security.

Specky for Eyes stores are well located on high streets, though these have suffered somewhat with a shift in consumer preference towards suburban shopping centres. None of Mr Specky's stores are located in these centres. However, with rising property prices, the current chain has seen rapidly increasing property values and, through limiting dividends, the cash balance is strong and borrowings negligible. The overall profit margins have suffered from increased competition, and the traditional product delivery methods have proven to be relatively more costly than competitors.

John Specky is married with two children, both now grown up. Neither has any interest in the business and, as John is rapidly approaching retirement, he is seeking advice on his strategic options. In recent years, a new COO has been hired from one of the business's competitors, as John has reduced his involvement in the business. The new COO is Bernadette Conway, an energetic entrepreneurial type. The handover of roles has worked out well so far, and she has expectations of becoming the new CEO shortly.

Bernadette has brought a breath of fresh air to the business with her drive to succeed and innovate, though this is not without its issues, as many staff resent the increased level of accountability she is demanding. Historically, all salaries were set centrally on the basis of a salary scale, on which staff would progress from one year to the next. A small bonus was paid at Christmas time, depending on the overall performance of the company, though this was not tied to any particular performance targets. Some of the store managers felt quite uneasy when Bernadette asked about performance goals for their stores.

Bernadette persuaded a well-known artist from a band called 'Too You' to endorse a range of glasses, and this has formed the basis for a new range of designer frames. Photos appeared in a range of well-known celebrity magazines and an advertising campaign is being planned.

The economy is, however, slowing down after many years of Celtic Tiger growth in consumer spending and is shrinking rapidly as the general public become more cost conscious.

However, spending amongst 20 to 30-year-olds (so-called Generation Y) remains strong. This group have typically found themselves still living at home, without any significant mortgage and are happy to rely on their credit cards as needed.

Bernadette indicates that her first priority is to increase the profitability of the stores. She comments that individual store profitability varies significantly — she refers you to a schedule (not provided), which compares the performance of two stores over recent months, as an example. She realises that there are significant challenges to getting the business and its staff to adopt a more positive approach to change.

As part of the drive for change, Bernadette hired a number of non-national opticians. As their qualifications were not recognised within the EU, it was possible to recruit them at very competitive rates. Typically, these new members of staff come to Ireland on a short visitor visa and then return home. Bernadette indicates that this has proven an effective way to introduce new services on a cost-effective basis.

John Specky and his wife Jacinta are the sole shareholders of Specky for Eyes Ltd. John is considering the possibility of retiring in the very near future and, in order to improve his golf handicap, moving to his summer home outside Wexford where he can avail of a range of local golf courses.

Specky for Eyes is an audit and tax client of your firm. You are now working for Harry O'Neill the Corporate Finance partner.

Case Study: Black & White Foods (BWF)

Black & White Foods Limited (BWF) has grown from a small family-owned company that produced black and white pudding (hence the name) into a major food ingredients company, and one of the five largest food colourant businesses in the world. It remains very much an Irish company, with each of its three production facilities in Ireland (Dublin, Cork and Belfast), using Irish ingredients where possible, and with all of the senior management team being not only Irish but also having progressed through the company, as BWF has a policy of 'promotion from within'.

The company is primarily owned by the Stanley family, the original creators of the company, and the family and attendant trusts have 68% of the equity. The current Managing Director, Jim Stanley, who is 62, personally owns 12% of the equity as part of the family stake and says that he and a number of other family members who work in the business realise the family ownership model will almost inevitably have to change within the next generation if BWF is to continue to grow. Jim makes it clear, however, that not all of the family members share his views on ownership of the business. Of the remaining equity in the business, a stake of 20% is owned by one of the largest Irish venture capital companies, who have been investors for 12 years and continue to be supportive of BWF. The remaining 12% is held by other key members of management, none of whom are Stanley family by birth, but some of whom are married to Stanley family members.Aw

As a newly-qualified Chartered Accountant, you started with BWF last week as Financial Analyst and have recently spent two hours with Jim Stanley discussing the 'big issues' affecting BWF, as Jim puts it. Jim started the meeting by explaining that the main reason that you got the job was your obvious interest in global business issues evident from your CV (based heavily on the overseas secondments you availed of as part of your training contract) and the covering letter with your application, together with your lack of any connections with either the auditors or separate business advisors to BWF, or any family connections. The Managing Director went on to say that BWF is a conservative company, both in its outlook, its financial practices and in its management style. Jim made the point that the top 20 people in the company have been with BWF for an average of 25 years each, and while this culture has served BWF well to date, he realises they will have to become more outward-looking and globally-focused going forward, hence this new Financial Analyst role.

Jim says he wishes he had an organisational chart to show you, but explains that the company is organised in a very traditional way, along functional lines, with eight directors of Finance, Sales, Marketing, R&D, Personnel, Transport and Logistics, Production, and Quality Control all reporting directly to Jim. These nine people, including Jim, along with the eight deputy directors and the three location production managers make up a 20-person Key Management Group (KMG). The Group meets formally every fortnight, in each of the three different production locations in line with a rolling schedule drawn up at least 18 months in advance, which is rigidly adhered to, such that holidays are planned so that either a functional director, or his or her deputy, is always present for meetings of the KMG. You have been given the KMG schedule and told that you are expected to attend forthcoming meetings, and may be required to present your findings at short notice, so it is important they are prepared in bullet point format that can easily be translated into PowerPoint slides.

Jim provides you with the financial details contained in Appendix 1, which were tabled recently at the KMG, and makes the point that although he (Jim) is a food scientist rather than an accountant, he understands that BWF is more than averagely profitable and is in a comfortable financial position, making the point that "even if I knew nothing about accounts, the fact that bankers keep inviting me to seminars in Switzerland and to private golf events would convince me I am not borrowing enough for their wishes". Making the point that most of the KMG agenda deals with operational matters, Jim also said that the KMG recently considered a formal mission statement for BWF and eventually gave up because everybody contributed something from their function and it became far too long. However, the essence of what they were trying to get to was that BWF would remain an international leader in foods by focusing at all times on innovation and quality, and that they would actively seek to minimise risk, given some of the spectacular business failures they had seen recently.

By focusing solely on a niche within the food ingredients business – colourants that are safe to eat – BWF has been remarkably successful, even within the context of the food ingredients business. The food ingredients business generally has shown above average growth in the last 20 years. BWF has rapidly become one of the top five colourant companies in the world, and the largest in Europe. It is headquartered just outside Dublin, where its main production plant is located and where all Research and Development (R&D) is concentrated. BWF has satellite manufacturing plants, one in Cork and the other in Belfast. BWF has sales of €220 million.

Although BWF is in a strong position in its niche, colourings, by their nature, form only a tiny part of the ingredients cost of ready-prepared food. A company in broader food ingredients (such as pasta, rice, vegetables, meats) in a similar market position and geographical segment to BWF would have a turnover of at least US$2 billion, or six to seven times the size of BWF. Two of the five main competitors of BWF are part of large food ingredient businesses, but the customers of BWF are not in the food ingredient business for the vast majority of sales, but are food manufacturers. BWF has achieved earnings growth in excess of 25% p.a. compound for the last eight years, has invested heavily in both pure research and targeted R&D, and is in a comfortable cash position with minimal borrowings. BWF would make an expensive acquisition target for any publicly quoted company.

BWF has a huge product range in both natural colourants and synthesized colourants. These are stable products and customer relationships in this business tend to be long term. Because colourants represent only a tiny proportion of material costs, and because quality control and the absence of adverse reactions to other ingredients are so important, there is relatively little competition on price. The opportunity to gain new customers tends to come from either persistently having a superior product in a particular colour, or less typically from investing in a new product ideally suited to an emerging food trend. BWF has gained customers primarily because of its better, more stable product. Six months ago, Jim commissioned an economic consulting firm and a consumer advertising agency to work together to identify the coming trends in food consumption. He took this approach rather than using a market research agency, to try to get some unique insights into what his customers were doing, and how this was changing, and this paper was presented to the KMG. Jim has provided you with a summary of their findings, set out below.

The Report on Future Trends

The work identified the following trends:

1. *Consumer Dynamics*

    - Consumer demands and expectations continue to rise
    - Palates have become increasingly demanding
    - Cooking is a low priority chore
    - Restaurant quality food has become the benchmark
    - Brand power increasingly drives purchases
    - The recession has not significantly impacted processed food volumes at all, people continue to eat prepared foods, though there is some evidence of price resistance at retail level

2. *Streamlining and Simplifying Business Infrastructure*

    - Food manufacturers are retaining only critical processes in the value chain and outsourcing others
    - Food businesses must originate, formulate and market products constantly and quickly

3. *Consolidation*

    - Spending on R&D by food multinationals has fallen as a percentage of sales
    - Specialist ingredient companies are driving R&D
    - Major food companies are entering partnership arrangements

4. *Shift from Food Manufacture to Food Assembly*

    - Food companies look to their preferred supplier partners for procurement of value added components

5. Growth of Foodservice at Expense of Retail

- 'Quick service restaurants' will account for 85% of "home meal replacement" in next 5 years
- Food service entities have become global
- Europe is behind the US, but growing quicker at 20% p.a.

6. Globalisation of Menus and Food Companies

- Consumers are exposed to an ever-growing range of fusion flavours, where techniques are taken from more than one cuisine to create new dishes
- The food industry has responded through the development of global brands and products

7. Convenient Consumption

- "Street food" and "round-the-clock" food service will become increasingly attractive for snack consumption and "on-the-go" demands
- In the US, over 18% of food is now consumed in cars

8. Niche Markets

- Growth of ethnic population segments is increasing demand for authentic ethnic foods

At their last meeting, KMG looked at the possible acquisition of a food manufacturer, Food2Fly, as part of a strategy to diversify the dependence of BWF on colourants, and a summary of the background report on Food2Fly prepared by Phoenix & Co. (an advisory firm who have done satisfactory work for BWF before) is presented as Appendix 2. The KMG were deeply divided on such an acquisition, with the production and operations directors opposed to any such diversification, and most others feeling that any such strategic move should only be considered in light of a better analysis of the external environment and the place of BWF in such an environment.

The marketing director noted that, according to the Minutes of the KMG, they had within the past six months separately considered the following strategic options, each of which had some merits from his perspective:

- BWF could develop cross-shareholding links with a larger food ingredients group
- BWF could become a larger food supplies group itself, principally by the acquisition of companies such as (but not limited to) Food2Fly
- BWF could use its financial strength and the depressed state of the property market to begin to build up a property portfolio as a bulwark against any downturn in the main food business
- BWF could stay focused on edible colourants and aim to reduce its business and financial risk.

Jim has, therefore, asked you to address the following:

(**Note**: Suggested solutions to these Exercises are at the end of this text.)

BWF Case – Exercise 1

Provide the Board with fresh insights into the external environment facing BWF.

Student Guidance In preparing this exercise, students could use the following tools to analyse the external environment of the company:

- PEST analysis
- Porter's Five Forces
- Porter's Diamond
- Opportunities and Threats from the SWOT analysis model

(These tools are discussed in **Gallagher**, in Chapters 5 and 6.)

It is clear from your terms of reference from the MD that the KMG do not want a theoretical, academic exercise but rather a structured, bullet point professional assessment of the positive and negative factors in the external environment, both now and in the future.

In terms of a suggested methodology, the best approach is first to revise the tools needed to complete the exercise, principally those set out above. The revision of these tools will in itself typically prompt some ideas on the external environment of BWF. You may then want to review any notes, articles or other material you have on the food industry to augment the Report of Future Trends you have been given above. At that stage, you should be in a position to generate a list of possible points, which can then be assessed for their relevance or otherwise to BWF, and then ranked in terms of their relative importance. At this stage, you can then draft the answer to the exercise, making sure that the points are not generic but are specifically relevant to BWF.

When elaborating on the points, bear in mind the constraints imposed by the need for this work to form the basis for a PowerPoint presentation. A key aspect of Competence will be the suitability of the solution for translation into a PowerPoint presentation, as specifically requested by KMG.

(A Suggested Solution to this Exercise is at the end of this text.)

BWF Case – Exercise 2

Distil your analysis of BWF into five key competencies or strategic strengths of the company and use your analysis of the external environment to identify specific future threats to each of these current competencies, as well as opportunities to further develop these key competencies.

Student Guidance In preparing the first part of this exercise (identification of the key competencies), students should revise their notes on competitive position and competitive advantage dealt with in *Gallagher*, Chapter 6.

Having revised this area, you should then review the case material presented to identify the key competencies required.

Note that you are specifically asked for five key competencies, and this is in line with the approach of the Key Management Group of BWF, which is to look for information in a bullet point format. The ability to present information in such a format is a key competency in both this exercise and in real life, and this will be reflected in the assessment methodology. What this means in practice for the student is that only the first five competencies will be assessed, irrespective of how many are listed, or in what order they are listed.

Having identified the five key competencies, students should then revisit their analysis of the external environment prepared in Exercise 1, extracting the key opportunities and threats, and match these opportunities and threats to the key competencies. You should expect to see every opportunity and threat matched to at least one key competency; if they do not affect one of the key competencies, it is hard to see how they could be regarded as a significant opportunity or threat as their impact on the competitive position of BWF is clearly limited. In this way, Exercise 2 serves as a check on Exercise 1 and it is possible that, following the completion of Exercise 2, you may decide to revise or re-order your answer to Exercise 1. Likewise, you should expect that each key competency will have at least one risk and one opportunity assigned to it. In the absence of such a matching of competencies with risks and opportunities, you may need to look again at the completeness of your listing of opportunities and threats in Exercise 1.

The solution should clearly be presented in tabular, bullet point format, with three columns, one for key competencies and one each for matching opportunities and threats.

(A Suggested Solution to this Exercise is at the end of this text.)

BWF Case – Exercise 3
  (a) Rank the relative attractiveness of the four identified strategic options on the basis of their responsiveness to the external environment and their ability to build on the key competencies identified.
  (b) Identify other strategic options that the KMG should consider.
  (c) Set out an action plan and timeframe for the KMG to allow them to conclude on the strategic options that they should adopt.

Student Guidance The four strategic options considered by the KMG have been explained by the Marketing Director in the case. You have been given two criteria on which to rank the four options and, before completing the ranking, you should review the opportunities and threats in the external environment from Exercise 1 and the five key competencies from Exercise 2. The ranking process is quite straightforward, using a measure of 4 for the strategic option that best avails of the opportunities in the external environment and avoids the threats identified, a measure of 3 for the next best, and so on, with the same exercise to be performed in terms of a match with the key competencies from Exercise 2. This gives a maximum score of 8 and a minimum of 2, with the highest score having the highest ranking.

In terms of identifying other strategic options that the KMG should consider and the appropriate time frame and action plan, students should first review *Gallagher* Chapters 9 and 10 on developing strategic options.

In terms of setting out the action plan and timeframe that the KMG should consider, students should first review Chapter 8 of this Toolkit.

(A Suggested Solution to this Exercise is at the end of this text.)

BWF Case – Exercise 4

Set out the actions that BWF will need to take as part of a medium-term business plan in the light of your analysis above. As part of this exercise, draft the executive summary of a business plan for BWF designed in part to raise additional bank debt or equity for the company.

Student Guidance This exercise requires you to review the analysis of BWF carried out to date and decide on the medium-term planning implications of those actions. For example, enhancing the capability of BWF in the area of R&D if that is regarded as a key competency of the company that needs to be reinforced.

The second part of the exercise requires you to identify the key aspects of the financial position and prospects of BWF that can be presented to a lender or investor in a positive yet balanced way.

In terms of setting out the actions BWF should consider, students should first review Chapter 8 of this Toolkit.

For advice on how to draft an executive summary, students should review the Example Business Plan contained in Chapter 8 of this Toolkit.

(A Suggested Solution to this Exercise is at the end of this text.)

BWF Case – Exercise 5

Evaluate the strengths and weaknesses of the current organisational model adopted by BWF, and suggest changes to make it more responsive to the business environment in which BWF operates.

Student Guidance Students should, in the first instance, review *Gallagher*, Chapters 2, 7 and 14 on organisational structure, culture and management style, noting the advantages and disadvantages of the traditional functional organisational model, and the alternative structures available. Students should then review the information given in relation to the model adopted by BWF and the analyses of the external environment and the company in Exercises 1 and 2 above, and conclude on whether the organisational model currently in place in BWF needs to change and, if so, what those changes should be.

(A Suggested Solution to this Exercise is at the end of this text.)

Appendix 1 – Selected Financial Highlights of Black & White Foods Limited – Financial Year Ending 30 June

All Figures €/£ millions	2009	2008	2007	2006	2005
Revenues	**220**	**198**	**176**	**159**	**143**
Gross margin	66	58	49	46	42
R&D costs	12	10	8	6	5
Other expenses excluding interest	31	28	25	23	20
Interest	1	2	3	4	4
Net profit before tax	**22**	**18**	**13**	**13**	**13**
Tax	4	3	2	2	2
Net profit after tax	**18**	**15**	**11**	**11**	**11**
Dividends	1	1	1	1	1
Retained earnings	17	14	10	10	10
Net assets	**180**	**163**	**149**	**139**	**129**
Borrowings	16	28	40	46	50

Appendix 2 – Briefing Notes on Food2Fly Limited prepared by Phoenix & Co., advisors to Black & White Foods Limited (Private and Confidential)

Food2Fly Limited (F2F) is owned by a husband and wife team, Steve and Betty Barclay. It grew and prospered from a base in a high quality catering service. Twenty years ago Steve and Betty decided, almost on a whim, to enter a tendering competition for the major airline serving the local international market to provide pre-cooked food for its first class service. They were encouraged in this by a senior executive in the airline, who had been a personal customer of their catering service. While helpful in terms of background, he had no role in purchasing and they won the tender fair and square. They did not have the cheapest tender, but won on the basis of the best and most innovative menu, which they undertook to change significantly more often than the tender conditions demanded.

While this win represented a huge increase in volume, premises were not an issue, as food was then cooked in a kitchen at the airport, blast frozen in bulk before loading on the plane, reheated in large trays and portioned up by stewardesses in a specially designed galley. The position now is different, in that the food is prepared away from the airport in commercial kitchens, portioned up, and the entire tray prepared with the hot food element, if any, being supplied in individual dishes to be reheated on the plane and combined with the rest of the tray in a much simplified galley. The emphasis now is on pre-production of the entire meal by F2F and similar companies, including the use of disposable plates, cutlery, etc. where possible. However, the process remains labour intensive, and it has been increasingly difficult and expensive to source staff.

The major airline for whom F2F worked initially was one of the first to contract out the preparation of in-flight food, but this approach has been taken by almost all major airlines for the last five years at least.

In general, F2F has been very successful, with a very high reputation for quality. They now serve all international airports on the island of Ireland and many, but not all, airlines flying from these airports. They have at least 70% of the market in terms of food loaded onto planes, with the rest spread between broadly equal competitors. Of the three competitors, one is locally owned, one is owned by an international food services group and the third is owned by an airline, which itself does not have a big presence on the routes on and off the island.

However, FY 2008 and FY 2009 have been very poor for F2F. There was margin pressure anyway, as the major airlines tried to cut costs to compete with the low-cost carriers, and volumes were down due to the economic downturn and the rise in fuel costs in FY 2008. This trend continued into FY 2009 and volume in Q4 FY 2009 fell by 40% compared to Q4 FY 2007. They also suffered a bad debt of €/£100,000 in respect of an African airline for whom they did some subcontract work in FY 2009.

While volumes are expected to pick up a little in the early part of FY 2010, there is still intense pressure on margins. Steve and Betty have decided to take a radical look at the business, especially in the light of global trends, and feel they really need to be part of a larger food group that is more in touch with developments in the food industry.

Food2Fly Limited: Selected Financial Highlights – Financial Year Ends 30 June

Financial year	2009	2008	2007	2006	2005	2004	2003
Servings (000s)							
– Prestige (1)	100	170	200	180	150	120	100
– Premium (1)	1,700	1,930	2,100	1,920	1,750	1,580	1,200
– Classic (1)	1,900	1,900	1,800	1,600	1,600	1,500	1,400
Total	**3,700**	**4,000**	**4,100**	**3,700**	**3,500**	**3,200**	**2,700**
Sales (£/€000s)							
– Dublin	8,100	10,000	10,200	8,200	6,500	5,200	4,000
– Belfast	1,600	1,750	1,800	1,600	1,400	1,200	1,000
– Cork	1,000	1,100	1,200	1,000	850	750	600
– Knock	500	550	600	550	500	450	400
Total	**11,200**	**13,400**	**13,800**	**11,350**	**9,250**	**7,600**	**6,000**
Cost of Sales (£/€000s)							
Material	3,100	2,950	2,500	2,300	1,950	1,700	1,500
Labour	3,400	3,800	3,700	2,900	2,200	1,700	1,200
Internet costs	1,500	1,450	1,300	1,200	950	750	600
Total	8,000	8,200	7,500	6,400	5,100	4,150	3,300
Contribution (£/€000s)							
	3,200	5,200	6,300	4,950	4,150	3,450	2,700
Overheads							
Administration	2,400	2,100	1,800	1,500	1,300	1,200	1,100
Marketing/design	3,000	2,400	2,000	1,600	1,200	900	600
Finance	200	100	100	50	50	50	50
Total	5,600	4,600	3,900	3,150	2,550	2,150	1,750
Profit/(loss) before tax							
£/€000s	(2,400)	600	2,400	1,800	1,600	1,300	950
Operating cash flow	(1,600)	(400)	1,400	1,300	1,100	1,000	600
Capital Invest.	100	300	600	600	400	400	300
Wastage (2)	8%	5%	3%	1%	1%	2%	2%

Notes

(1)   From the start, F2F operated a menu system, and their catering experience led them to create three menus, each with a wide range of selections within them:

- **Prestige** – this is for first/business class customers and includes premium hot food, non-disposable plates and cutlery, fresh juices, complimentary chocolate, etc.

- **Premium** – a number of airlines use this for business class, or give everyone the same menu. It includes a less extensive range of hot food, disposable plates and cutlery, and less use of extras to dress up the meal.

- **Classic** – this is widely used, but not by most of the 'low-cost' airlines which do not provide any in-flight food as part of the price of a ticket. This represents an unheated meal (cereal or salad essentially) and is significantly cheaper per unit, as well as being easier for both F2F and the airline to handle. It significantly reduces the need for galley space.

(2)   Under the contracts with the airlines, which tend to be negotiated for a period of at least a year, F2F will be responsible for a portion of the unused servings put on board. These are effectively scrapped afterwards. These unused servings arise because of:

- **Allowing for choice** – the more choice given, the greater the wastage, as you have to allow for the fact that a customer's choice will not be spread equally over the options available.
- **Spillages, etc.,** which are inevitable.
- **Fluctuating passenger numbers** – as the food has to be prepared in advance, and then delivered to the airport in good time, F2F bases its numbers on the seats booked up to 18 hours before the flight by phoning the airline, and must err on the side of caution. When flights are full, that does not matter, but in 2008 and 2009 this has become an increasing problem as load factors have fallen on all airlines. F2F does not bear all the cost – it is negotiated as part of the contract – but it is typically at least 50%.

Google Inc. – One Decade Later

Theodore Lynn, Louise Gorman, Malcolm Brady

> "Our mission is to organize the world's information and make it universally accessible and useful. We believe that the most effective, and ultimately the most profitable, way to accomplish our mission is to put the needs of our users first."[1]

On 8 September 2008, Google celebrated their 10th anniversary. In those 10 years, Google had gone from a garage business to being one of the world's most powerful companies. In 2008, Google's revenues were $21.79 billion with a net income of $4.22 billion (see Exhibit 1).[2] They are the undisputed market leaders in search and Internet advertising and one of the world's most well-known brands (see Exhibit 2).[3]

2008 was also Google's fifth anniversary in Ireland. Their Irish Googleplex employs over 1,500 staff and is the Operations Headquarters for Europe, the Middle East and Africa. Google Ireland has consistently been voted one of the best companies to work for.[4] Like Google employees throughout the world, Googlers in Ireland enjoy excellent health and medical packages, free food and soft drinks, and other perks associated with working for one of the most in-demand employers worldwide.[5]

Over its first decade, Google experienced phenomenal success relatively unchallenged. However, clouds are beginning to emerge on the horizon. Existing competitors are beginning to team up against them, new competitors are challenging their technical dominance, regulators are increasingly focusing on their dominant position, and arguably their greatest assets, their user base and their employees, are beginning to question whether the company whose motto is famously "Don't be evil" is turning into the Evil Empire.

---

[1] Google Annual Report 2008, Page 1 -
http://investor.google.com/pdf/2008_google_annual_report.pdf
[2] Google Annual Report 2008, Page 66 -
http://investor.google.com/pdf/2008_google_annual_report.pdf
[3] Millward Brown Optimor, *The Brandz Top 100 Most Valuable Global Brands 2009*,
http://www.millwardbrown.com/Sites/optimor/Media/Pdfs/en/BrandZ/BrandZ-2009-Report.pdf
[4] Great Places to Work, http://www.greatplacetowork.com/best/search-results.php?
[5] Google Ireland Jobs, http://www.google.ie/support/jobs/bin/static.py?page=why-dub.html

The Evolution of the Google Business Model – Search and Advertising

Larry Page (24) and Sergey Brin (23) first met in the summer of 1995 at Stanford University when Sergey was assigned to show Larry around as he considered studying at the university. While, according to some, they did not hit it off at first, in 1996 they eventually began working together as graduate students on a search engine project codenamed "Backrub".

In the early 1990s, search services had evolved from human-generated directories to automated search that used "spiders" to create an index of web page contents, and algorithms to rank page relevance based on the frequency of keyword references. This had the unintended consequence of returning irrelevant listings, much of which could be attributed to "advertisers" taking measures to gain user attention through the manipulation of automated search engines.[6] This not only frustrated users but, because of the exponential growth of the World Wide Web, consumed a significant amount of time. Essentially, Backrub made use of the analysis of the number and type of references or links to a particular site to evaluate the quality of web pages and rank them in search results. In 1997, Backrub was renamed Google.

In September 1998 with $100,000 from Sun Microsystems co-founder Andy Bechtolsheim, Google Inc. was incorporated and they hired their first employee, Craig Silverstein, a fellow grad student at Stanford. By the end of the year, *PC Magazine* recognised Google as the search engine of choice in the Top 100 Web Sites for 1998.[7] In June 1999, Google announced the completion of a $25 million round of equity funding led by Sequoia Capital and Kleiner Perkins Caufield & Byers, two of the leading venture capital companies in the US.[8] A year later, Google replaced Inktomi as Yahoo's default search provider.[9] In less than two years, Google Inc. was the world's largest search engine with over one billion URLs.[10]

Google's revenue model was limited to fees generated through licensing their search technology to third parties such as Yahoo. At the beginning of 1999, Google's website, www.google.com, reflected their corporate values (see Exhibit 3) with a very simple user-friendly design with no advertising, even in the search engine results page. Unlike their competition, Google saw their role as a technology company with their users as the focus. As such, while other websites and portals sought to retain "eyeballs" with content and functionality to generate advertisement revenue, content on www.google.com was restricted to search results and limited company

---

[6] Brin, S. and Page, L., The Anatomy of a Large-Scale Hypertextual Web Search Engine, http://infolab.stanford.edu/~backrub/google.html

[7] PC Magazine Online, Top 100 Websites - http://web.archive.org/web/19990508042436/www.zdnet.com/pcmag/special/web100/search2.html

[8] Google Receives $25 Million in Equity Funding - http://web.archive.org/web/20000309205910/http://google.com/pressrel/pressrelease1.html

[9] Yahoo! Selects Google as its Default Search Engine Provider - http://www.google.com/press/pressrel/pressrelease25.html

[10] Google Launches World's Largest Search Engine - http://www.google.com/press/pressrel/pressrelease26.html

information. Other search engines and portals, namely Yahoo, MSN and AOL, generated substantial revenues by displaying paid listings adjacent to or interspersed with search results.

At this time, the paid listings market was dominated by Overture. Their model relied on advertisers bidding for keywords, with the relative bid amount determining the ordering of ads on the search engine results page – advertisers paid only when users clicked on their paid listing. This model was very popular with advertisers as a large percentage of web searches had a commercial motivation and the "cost per click" (CPC) auction model met both user and advertiser needs. Users, typically, clicked on the highest ordered ads and those advertisers who paid most were ordered closer to the top and would probably generate greater revenues if they matched a searcher's needs.

In October 2000, Google launched AdWords with 350 customers. AdWords was a self-service advertisement programme with online activation with a credit card, keyword targeting and performance feedback.[11] Success for Google would depend on beating the competition on coverage rates, click through rates, average CPC and revenue splits. For the first time, Google was able to monetise the significant user traffic to their site. This gave Google a significant advantage over Overture which was dependent on network affiliates for coverage. While initially Google priced their ads on a fixed cost per impression basis, by 2002 they had adopted a variant of Overture's more successful model. Using a more sophisticated weighting system, Google introduced more relevancy for users to its paid listings, resulting in greater advertiser satisfaction and revenue maximisation. In addition, Google had a lower average CPC than Overture and paid more revenue to network affiliates.[12] By the end of 2002, Google was available in 26 languages, had over three billion documents in its index and over 24 million unique monthly visitors.[13] Strategic alliances such as those with Yahoo!, AOL and Universo Online, the largest Internet Service Provider in South America, drove more and more traffic and associated revenue.[14] Unlike Overture, Google was able to provide partners with search technology and paid listings and, by 2003, Google had caught up with Overture's first mover advantage.

Google began to take the lead in the paid listings market in March 2003 with the introduction of a content-targeted advertising service, also referred to as contextual paid listings. Contextual paid listings applied the precision of search advertising to the rest of the web; Google identified the meaning of a web page and then automatically served relevant ads. This service extended advertiser reach, provided users with highly relevant ads, and enabled website publishers to monetise content pages – even remnant or run-of-site inventory.[15] In April 2003 Google

---

[11] Google Launches Self-Service Advertising Program - http://www.google.com/press/pressrel/pressrelease39.html

[12] C. Bartley and S. Weinstein, "High growth in search creates opportunities for niche players", *Pacific Crest Securities*, 4 November, 2003.

[13] Google Corporate Information - http://www.google.com/corporate/history.html

[14] Google Becomes Premier Search Engine for Latin America- http://www.google.com/press/pressrel/uol.html

[15] Google Builds World's Largest Advertising and Search Monetisation Program - http://www.google.com/press/pressrel/advertising.html

acquired Applied Semantics and, together with the pre-existing content-targeting technology, this was rebranded AdSense. With a technical lead, a customer base of over 100,000 advertisers and serving 200 million searches, Google had the world's largest advertising and search monetisation programme.[16] The writing was on the wall for Overture. Since 2003, Google has gone on to dominate the online advertising market and in 2008 acquired one of its previous competitors, DoubleClick.[17]

Up to the end of 2004, Google products fell into two major categories, search or advertising, and this is borne out in their annual reports from the time.[18] This changed in 2005 when they listed software applications as part of their product portfolio for the first time.[19] Google's software portfolio included communication and collaboration tools and dowloadable applications. The former included Gmail (webmail), Orkut (social networking) and Blogger (blogging). The latter included Google Toolbar (browser application plug-in), Google Earth (virtual globe), Picasa (photo management) and Google Pack (free software bundle). Google also listed enterprise and mobile versions of popular Google search services. Google have continued unabated in to the software segment adding an online payment system, Google Checkout, and a raft of other applications to their portfolio. In 2006, it introduced one of its most significant software products, Google Apps, a suite of applications that includes Gmail webmail services, Google Calendar shared calendaring, Google Talk instant messaging and voice-over-IP, and the Personalised Start Page feature for creating a customisable home page on a specific domain. It has been extended to include Google Docs and Spreadsheets, which compete with Microsoft Office. There is a standard free service supported by paid listings, generated by automated scanning of email content. Google has also introduced a free education edition and more recently a premium edition for corporate users. In 2008, Google launched its own Internet browser, Google Chrome.[20]

Google's user base has grown largely by word of mouth. It comprises users, advertisers and content owners (who provide advertising space for Google Network). Google's marketing efforts have focused on feeding this word-of-mouth momentum and using public relations efforts to accelerate it. Google has significant sales and support infrastructure, with 32 sales offices in 19 countries, primarily to service their advertisers and content providers.[21] Today, 97% of Google's revenues are generated from advertising, with nearly a third of revenues

---

[16] Google Builds World's Largest Advertising and Search Monetisation Program - http://www.google.com/press/pressrel/advertising.html

[17] Google Closes Acquisition of DoubleClick - http://www.google.com/int/en/press/pressrel/20080311_doubleclick.html

[18] Google Annual Report 2004, Pages 4-9 - http://investor.google.com/pdf/2004_google_annual_report.pdf

[19] Google Annual Report 2005, Page 8 - http://investor.google.com/pdf/2005_google_annual_report.pdf

[20] Google Chrome: A New Take on the Browser http://www.google.com/int/en/press/pressrel/20080902_chrome.html

[21] Google Annual Report 2008, Page 14 - http://investor.google.com/pdf/2008_google_annual_report.pdf

attributable to Google's own websites.[22] The remaining revenues are generated from licensing and other activities. These include the sale and licence of the Google Search Appliance, and fees generated from Google TV Ads, Google Audio Ads, DoubleClick, Google Checkout, and Google Apps. None of these are material, although some use a significantly different business model than Google's main advertising business.[23] For example, Google Apps uses a Software-as-a-Service business model for business email, information sharing and security. Revenue is generated using a user-based subscription model. Google Checkout is an online shopping payment processing system for which Google receives transaction fees.

Product Development at Google

"Google Labs is a playground where our more adventurous users can play around with prototypes of some of our wild and crazy ideas and offer feedback directly to the engineers who developed them. Please note that Labs is the first phase in a lengthy product development process and none of this stuff is guaranteed to make it onto Google.com. While some of our crazy ideas might grow into the next Gmail or iGoogle, others might turn out to be, well, just plain crazy."[24]

Google's product development philosophy involves rapid and continuous innovation, with frequent releases of early-stage products that are then iterated and improved. Google engineers are encouraged to spend up to 20% of their time on an approved project of their choice. As ideas develop, more resources are allocated to the projects and those that percolate to the top may be released to Google Labs for live testing, google.com or other live test sites. If users find a product useful, Google may promote it to "beta" status for additional testing and ultimately make it a core product. These ideas typically fall into three categories: search and personalisation, advertising services, and software tools and services.

Google is committed to providing the most relevant and useful search results possible, independent of financial incentives. New developments in product search largely revolve around improving search performance and expanding in to new search domains. Improving search performance requires a constant refinement of search algorithms and evaluating new or potential breakthroughs in computer science to deliver better results. Over the last decade, Google has introduced the capability to conduct more complex queries, personalised search, web page translation, search by number, and cached links, to name but a few refinements. In 2008 alone, Google made 359 changes to their web search.[25] Google has also extended search in to new domains, including images (Image Search, 2001), news (News, 2002), products (Froogle, 2002), books (Google Print, 2003), personal hard drives (Desktop Search, 2004), academic publications (Scholar, 2004), publishable documents (Base, 2005), listings (Local, 2005), video (Video Search, 2005), financial information (Google Finance, 2006), patents (Patent Search, 2006), individual websites (Site Search, 2008) and even friends (Friend Connect, 2008).

---

[22] Google Annual Report 2008, Page 69
[23] Google Annual Report 2008, Pages 70-71
[24] Google Labs FAQ - http://www.googlelabs.com/faq
[25] Google Annual Report 2008, Annual Letter

Similar to the search, Google is committed to providing the most relevant and useful advertising. This also requires a significant R&D effort to maintain Google's leadership position in the market. This includes enhancing the different elements in the advertising process, including introducing new ad formats, refining bidding practices, combating click fraud, and providing analysis and decision support tools to advertisers. In 2006, Google extended its online advertising model to traditional print advertising[26] and in 2007, television. Google Checkout, an online payment processing system, is integrated with AdWords to help advertisers attract more leads, convert leads to sales and process those sales.

Google believes information becomes more valuable when combined with information from other people. As such they meet their corporate mission by developing tools for users to create, share and communicate information. Their product development strategy for software has three themes: 1. communication, collaboration and communities, 2. downloadable applications, and 3. geographic services. Google software strategy is largely dependent on the continuing trend toward ubiquitous computing, bandwidth and storage, often referred to as cloud computing. Central to Google's software proposition is the provision of substantial computing resources to users at low or no cost and leveraging Google's considerable infrastructure. While Google do provide downloadable applications, these often are designed to pass information to the Internet and Google.

Recently, Google has been consolidating its position at the forefront of search, advertising and software for mobile telephony. Google released a specially formatted version of its web search in 2005. Since then it has launched Gmail, Google News, Maps, iGoogle and AdSense for mobile phones. In a significant strategic move, Google acquired, refined and released Android, the first open platform for mobile devices in 2007. As with its search and advertising businesses, Google has partnered strategically to bring these products to market with major alliances with leading mobile communications companies such as China Mobile, T-Mobile, HTC, Qualcomm, Motorola and others.[27] In September 2008, T-Mobile announced the G1, the first phone built on the Android operating system.[28] Google also has a range of software built for the Apple iPhone and iTouch.

Not everything has to be invented at Google. They have made over 50 strategic acquisitions to run as standalone web sites (and thereby increase coverage for search and advertising) and to support other internal projects (see Exhibit 4). Google's first acquisition was Deja.com's Usenet Discussion Service in 2001. This acquisition accelerated Google's index at the time by giving users a new Usenet search feature that enabled them to search and browse more than 500 million archived messages. Other acquisitions that extended Google's reach and advertising coverage include Pyra Labs (2003), creators of the popular blogging service, Blogger (2003),

---

[26] Google Announces TV Ads Trial -
http://www.google.com/intl/en/press/annc/tv_ads_trial.html
[27] Industry Leaders Announce Open Platform for Mobile Devices -
http://www.google.com/intl/en/press/pressrel/20071105_mobile_open.html
[28] The First Android-powered Phone -
http://googleblog.blogspot.com/2008/09/first-android-powered-phone.html

YouTube (2006), and DoubleClick (2008). The DoubleClick acquisition had the dual benefit of removing a competitor from the market. From a technology perspective, Google has focused on acquiring technology that is either a new domain for Google or accelerates existing projects, typically in advertising and software tools. In advertising, Applied Semantics (2003) and Urchin (2005) were acquired to support AdSense and Google Analytics. While Android (2005), Writely (2006), JotSpot (2006) and Keyhole (2004) were the foundations for Android, Google Docs, Google Sites and Google Earth respectively.

Not every product idea is successful, at least in Google terms. In January 2009 alone, Google decided to discontinue work on a number of products. Google Video is to be discontinued as YouTube Picasa Web Album already services the video upload and sharing segment of the market. Google Catalog Search, an OCR technology demonstrator that led to Google's Book Search has also been discontinued. At the 2009 Zeitgeist conference, Brin admitted that Google had lost some ground in the market for applications for those who work on a "per-second" basis to microblogging companies such as Twitter. As such, Dodgeball, a mobile social network acquired by Google, is being shut down. Last year after launching "Lively", a competing virtual world to Linden Labs' Second Life, Google decided to terminate the project. Other Google projects being terminated include Google Base (an online database for publications), Knol (a competitor to Wikipedia), Grand Central (an advanced telecommunications service) and Google Print Ads. Ironically, many of these projects had made reasonable traction for start-up projects, but did not meet Google's high quality or adoption levels.

Don't Be Evil: Values and Governance at Google

The company is run by a triumvirate of the founders, Larry Page (President – Technology), Sergey Brin (President – Products), and Eric Schmidt (CEO). They meet daily with one of them often making key strategic decisions and briefing the others later.[29] Together, the management team make all strategic decisions and lead from the top to create the Google culture. Google's "10 things" list the key tenets of the Google philosophy:

1. Focus on the user and all else will follow.
2. It's best to do one thing really, really well.
3. Fast is better than slow.
4. Democracy on the Web works.
5. You don't need to be at your desk to need an answer.
6. You can make money without doing evil.
7. There's always more information out there.
8. The need for information crosses all borders.

---

[29] "An Owner's Manual" for Google's Shareholders -
http://investor.google.com/ipo_letter.html

9. You can be serious without a suit.

10. Great just isn't good enough.[30]

This idealism and unconventional approach to business and management can manifest itself in different ways which can be unsettling for traditional investors and commentators. For example, Google operated a Dutch auction for its IPO on NASDAQ in 2004.[31] The Google flotation was seen as a success with commentators stating that the IPO accomplished the goals of the company's founders and worked well for investors.[32] Shares initially sold for c. $40, they are now worth more than $300, valuing the company at nearly $100 billion.

Google has over 20,000 employees, all of whom hold equity in the company. However, Google is also unusual for a listed technology company because it has a dual-class equity structure. The rights of Class A and Class B common stock are identical, except with respect to voting. While the former is entitled to one vote per share, the latter is entitled to 10 votes per share. While institutional investors have significant financial stake in Google, the founders and CEO own approximately 90% of outstanding Class B common stock, representing approximately 68% of the voting power.[33] Critics have commented that this equity structure has "guaranteed that insiders will have 'carte blanche' authority in running the company."[34] The founders explained their rationale for the dual class structure as creating a structure designed for stability over long-time horizons and to allow the company and its management team to advance the company's core values, independent of fluctuations in quarterly results (see Exhibit 5).[35]

The Google values also permeate the working environment at Google. Employees don't work in an office but a Googleplex. They dress casually and have free food and soft drinks on-demand. There are areas to chill out in and games to play. Google attracts the best and they are paid well to work there. Googlers are there to change the world … and that means working hard, really hard.

---

[30] Google Corporate Information -
http://www.google.com/intl/en/corporate/tenthings.html
[31] Prior to the IPO, prospective investors, large and small, could bid for the number of shares and price at which they would be willing to purchase those shares. The final IPO price was determined after the auction closed when the underwriters calculated it by gathering all the bids and calculating the cut off point at or above which all the shares available could be sold.
[32] Google Dutch auction IPO declared a success -
http://www.vnunet.com/vnunet/news/2125714/google-dutch-auction-ipo-declared-success
[33] Google Annual Report 2008, Page 30 -
http://investor.google.com/pdf/2008_google_annual_report.pdf
[34] Kawamato, D., "Google gets low marks for governance", CNET, 23 August, 2004 -
http://news.cnet.com/Google-gets-low-marks-for-governance/2100-1030_3-5321813.html
[35] "An Owner's Manual" for Google's Shareholders -
http://investor.google.com/ipo_letter.html

Competitors

Google consider their primary competitors to be Microsoft and Yahoo. They compete for users, advertisers and content providers, but also for talent. Google's entry into Microsoft's core markets, combined with Yahoo's deteriorating market position and potential alliance with Microsoft, has intensified the rivalry between Microsoft and Google. As well as traditionally competing with Microsoft's MSN in the advertising space, Google has emerged as Microsoft's major competitor in email services (Gmail), productivity software (Google Apps) and more recently Internet browser software (Google Chrome) and mobile operating systems (Android).

But Microsoft and Yahoo are not Google's only competitors; it could be argued that Google are taking on nearly every major Web property with varying degrees of success and increasing mobile telephony leaders too. YouTube and Google Print have placed them in a competition with many of their content providers. Blogger, Orkut and Personalized HomePage, combined with Google Apps, compete with popular social networking tools and portals such as Yahoo!, Facebook and MySpace. Google Checkout extends their rivalry with Microsoft but also with companies such as eBay's PayPal.

Possibly more worrying for Google are the computer scientists and entrepreneurs seeking to outperform Google in their home territory, search. Although more than half of their revenues are generated outside of the US, they are not the market leader in a number of key markets including South Korea, China, Russia and Japan.[36] As well as smaller domain- and market-specific competitors (see Exhibit 6), some commentators believe that Google are about to face their first significant challenges for technology leadership in the web search space. While Google provided significantly more relevant search results than the previous generation of web search technology, the results are far from perfect. Google may make the world's information available, but can the information presented in Google's results be trusted? Do they provide users with insight? A new company, WolframAlpha, the Web's first "computational knowledge engine", claims to have made significant advances in this area. Launched in May 2009, WolframAlpha only holds factual data and a lot of it. On its launch, users can access over 10 trillion pieces of information sourced from thousands of official websites, libraries and academic journals, and checked by experts.[37] To make matters worse, on 28 May 2009 Microsoft unveiled Bing, a new "Decision Engine" which they claim moves beyond search to help customers make better decisions, focusing initially on four key vertical areas: making a purchase decision, planning a trip, researching a health condition or finding a local business.[38]

---

[36] Freedman, D., "Searching for the next Google", *Newsweek*, 5 November, 2007 - http://www.newsweek.com/id/62254

[37] Harris, M., "WolframAlpha: move over Google?", *Sunday Times*, 17 May 2009 - http://technology.timesonline.co.uk/tol/news/tech_and_web/article6294437.ece

[38] Microsoft's New Search at Bing.com Helps People Make Better Decisions - http://www.microsoft.com/presspass/press/2009/may09/05-28NewSearchPR.mspx

The Next Decade: Where now for Google?

As they enter their second decade, Google face a global economic recession. They are beginning to face some questions over technical leadership in the search domain and an alliance between Microsoft and Yahoo may threaten their dominance and existing deals in the online advertising market.[39] They are even losing key staff to rivals such as AOL and Twitter as claims in the media and blogosphere suggest that key staff feel underused and that Google is becoming the same as any other large business to work for.[40]

Increasingly questions are being asked about Google's ambitions. Regulators and activists have raised questions over their dominance in search and online advertising. Google's concession to the Chinese government to censor its Chinese service resulted in protests from the media, policymakers and indeed their own shareholders, many of whom are employees.[41] Contrarily, statements by Google management declaring that the company's goal is to collect as much data as it can on individual users to improve the quality of its products has raised the ire of right-to-privacy campaigners.[42]

As one of the world's largest companies, it is not surprising that Google is a target for law suits on a variety of fronts, from private companies and government agencies. Over its first decade, Google was challenged on a number of legal fronts including misleading and deceptive conduct (AdWords), trademark infringement (Adwords), copyright infringement (YouTube and Google Book Search), and right to privacy (Google Street View). It begins its second decade in the same vein. US regulators have taken up at least three inquiries related to Google since 2008. The US Justice Department has inquiries into both Google's search-advertising deal with Yahoo and Google's settlement with authors and publishers to gain copyright licences to millions of digitised works relating to Google Book Search.[43] The latter has raised similar concerns in Europe.[44] More recently, the US Federal Trade Commission is inquiring into whether an overlap of two directors on the boards of Google and Apple could violate antitrust laws by reducing competition.[45]

As Google enters the next decade, can they maintain their dominance in the search and advertising market and take on Microsoft? Can they continue to attract the top talent that has made them a success? Are they now the new "Microsoft" waiting for the next "Google" to knock on their door?

---

[39] Johnson, B., "Microsoft and Yahoo revive talks as Google leaps ahead", *The Guardian*, 10 April 2009 - http://www.guardian.co.uk/business/2009/apr/10/microsoft-yahoo-merger-talks

[40] Quinn, J., "Google searches out unhappy staff", *The Telegraph*, 20 May 2009 - http://www.telegraph.co.uk/finance/5352086/Google-searches-out-unhappy-staff.html

[41] MacMillan, D., "Google, Yahoo Criticized Over Foreign Censorship", *BusinessWeek*, 13 March 2009 - http://www.businessweek.com/technology/content/mar2009/tc20090312_381922.htm

[42] Arlidge, J., "Google. Who's looking at you?", *Sunday Times Magazine*, 21 October 2007 - http://technology.timesonline.co.uk/tol/news/tech_and_web/the_web/article2688404.ece

[43] Vascellaro, J.E. and Kane Y., "Apple, Google Scrutinized by FTC", *Wall Street Journal*, 5 May 2009 - http://online.wsj.com/article/SB124149161449086315.html

[44] Jones Huw, "EU to study how Google Books impact authors", Reuters, 28 May 2009 - http://www.reuters.com/article/technologyNews/idUSTRE54R5M420090528

[45] Vascellaro, J.E. and Kane, Y., "Apple, Google Scrutinized by FTC", *Wall Street Journal*, 5 May 2009 - http://online.wsj.com/article/SB124149161449086315.html

Exhibit I – Consolidated Income Statements of Google Inc., Yahoo Inc., and Microsoft Inc.

Google Consolidated Income Statements 2002–2008 (Figures in thousands of US Dollars, except per share amounts and EPS)

$000	2002	2003	2004	2005	2006	2007	2008
Revenues	439,508	1,465,934	3,189,223	6,138,560	10,604,917	16,593,986	21,795,550
Costs and Expenses							
Cost of Revenues	132,575	634,411	1,468,967	2,577,088	4,225,027	6,649,085	8,621,506
Research & Development	40,494	229,605	395,164	599,510	1,228,589	2,119,985	2,793,192
Sales & Marketing	48,783	164,935	295,749	468,152	849,518	1,461,266	1,946,244
General & Administrative	31,190	94,519	188,151	386,532	751,787	1,279,250	1,802,639
Settlement of dispute with Yahoo!	-	-	201,000	-	-	-	-
Contribution to Google Foundation	-	-	-	90,000	-	-	-
Total Costs & Expenses	253,042	1,123,470	2,549,031	4,121,282	7,054,921	11,509,586	15,163,581
Income from operations	186,466	342,464	640,192	2,017,278	3,549,996	5,084,400	6,631,969
Net Income	99,656	105,648	399,119	1,465,397	3,077,446	4,203,720	4,226,858
EPS (As reported)							
Basic	$ 0.86	$ 0.77	$ 2.07	$ 5.31	$ 10.21	$ 13.53	$ 13.46
Diluted	$ 0.45	$ 0.41	$ 1.46	$ 5.02	$ 9.94	$ 13.29	$ 13.31

Yahoo Consolidated Income Statements 2002–2008 (Figures in thousands of US Dollars, except per share amounts and EPS)

$000	2002	2003	2004	2005	2006	2007	2008
Revenues	953,067	1,625,097	3,574,517	5,257,668	6,425,679	6,969,274	7,208,502
Cost of Revenues	162,881	358,103	1,298,559	2,096,201	2,675,723	2,838,758	3,023,362
Gross Profit	790,186	1266994	2,275,958	3,161,467	3,749,956	4,130,516	4,185,140
Operating Expenses							
Sales & Marketing	429,968	530,613	778,029	1,033,947	1,322,259	1,610,357	1,563,313
Product development	141,766	207,285	368,760	569,527	833,147	1,084,238	1,221,787
General & Administrative	100,676	157,027	262,602	341,073	528,798	633,431	705,136
Stock Compensation Expense	8,402	22,029	32,290	-			
Amortization of Intangibles	21,186	54,374	145,696	109,195	124,786	107,077	705,136
Restructuring charges, net	-	-	-	-	-	-	106,854
Goodwill impairment charge	-	-	-	-	-	-	487,537
Total Operating Expenses	701,998	971,328	1,587,377	2,053,742	2,808,990	3,435,103	4,172,177
Income from Operations	88,188	295,666	688,581	1,107,725	940,966	695,413	12,963
Other Income, Net	69,287	47,506	496,443	1,435,857	157,034	154,011	82,838
Income before income taxes, earnings in equity interests, minor interests and cumulative effect of accounting change	157,475	343,172	1,185,034	2,543,582	1,098,000	849,424	95,801
Provision for income taxes	−71,290	−147,024	−437966	−767,816	−458,011	−337,263	−262,717
Earnings in equity interests	22,301	47,652	94,991	128,244	112,114	150,689	596,979
Minority interests in operations	−1,551	−5,921	−2,496	−7,780	−712	−2,850	−5,765
Net income before cumulative effect of accounting change	42,815	237,879	839,553	1,896,230	751,391	660,000	424,298
Cumulative effect of accounting change	−64,120	-	-	-	-	-	-
Net income	42,815	237,879	839,553	1,896,230	751,391	660,000	424,298

Net income per share – basic							
Net income per share before cumulative effect of accounting change	$0.09	$0.19	$0.62	$1.35	$0.54	$0.49	$0.31
Cumulative effect of accounting change per share	– $0.05	–	–	–	–	–	–
Net income per share – basic	$0.04	$0.19	$0.62	$1.35	$0.54	$0.49	$0.31
Net income per share – diluted							
Net income per share before cumulative effect of accounting change	$0.09	$0.18	$0.58	$1.28	$0.52	$0.47	$0.29
Net income per share – diluted	$0.04	$0.18	$0.58	$1.28	$0.52	$0.47	$0.29

Microsoft Consolidated Income Statements 2002–2008 (Figures in millions of US Dollars, except per share amounts and EPS)

$000,000	2002	2003	2004	2005	2006	2007	2008
Revenue	28,365	32,187	36,835	39,788	44,282	51,122	44,282
Operating Expenses							
Cost of revenue	5,699	6,059	6,716	6,031	7,650	10,693	7,650
Research and development	6,299	6,595	7,779	6,097	6,584	7,121	6,584
Sales and marketing	6,252	7,562	8,309	8,563	9,818	11,455	9,818
General and administrative	1,843	2,426	4,997	4,536	3,758	3,329	3,758
Total operating expenses	20,093	22,642	27,801	25,227	27,810	32,598	27,810
Operating income	8,272	9,545	9,034	14,561	16,472	18,524	16,472
Losses on equity investees and other	– 92	– 68	– 25	–	–	–	–
Investment income/(loss)	– 305	1,577	3,187	2,067	1,790	1,577	1,790
Income before income taxes	7,875	11,054	12,196	16,628	18,262	20,101	18,262
Provision for income taxes	2,520	3,523	4,028	4,374	5,663	6,036	5,663
Net income	5,355	7,531	8,168	12,254	12,599	14,065	12,599
Earnings per share:							
Basic	$0.50	$0.70	$0.76	$1.13	$1.21	$1.44	$1.21
Diluted	$0.48	$0.69	$0.75	$1.12	$1.20	$1.42	$1.20
Weighted average shares:							
Basic	10,811	10,723	10,803	10,839	10,438	9,742	10,438
Diluted	11,106	10,882	10,894	10,906	10,531	9,886	10,531

Exhibit 2 – Millward Brown Optimor Top 25 Most Valuable Global Brands 2009

#	Brand	Brand 2009 ($M)	% Brand Value Change 2009 vs. 2008
1	Google	100,039	16%
2	Microsoft	76,249	8%
3	Coca Cola	67,625	67,625
4	IBM	66,622	20%
5	McDonald's	66,575	34%
6	Apple	63,113	14%
7	China Mobile	61,283	7%
8	GE	59,793	− 16%
9	Vodafone	53,727	45%
10	Marlboro	49,460	33%
11	Walmart	41,083	19%
12	ICBC (Asia)	38,056	36%
13	Nokia	35,163	− 20%
14	Toyota	29,907	− 15%
15	UPS	27,842	− 9%
16	Blackberry	27,478	100%
17	HP	26,745	− 9%
18	BMW	23,948	− 15%
19	SAP	23,615	9%
20	Disney	23,110	− 3%
21	Tesco	22,938	− 1%
22	Gillette	22,919	6%
23	Intel	22,851	22,851
24	China Construction Bank	22,811	16%
25	Oracle	21,438	-6%

Exhibit 3 – Google Corporate Philosophy[46]

NEVER SETTLE FOR THE BEST

"The perfect search engine," says Google co-founder Larry Page, "would understand exactly what you mean and give back exactly what you want." Given the state of search technology today, that's a far-reaching vision requiring research, development and innovation to realise. Google is committed to blazing that trail. Although acknowledged as the world's leading search technology company, Google's goal is to provide a much higher level of service to all those who seek information, whether they're at a desk in Boston, driving through Bonn or strolling in Bangkok.

---

[46] Google Corporate Information - http://www.google.com/intl/en/corporate/tenthings.html

To achieve this, Google has persistently pursued innovation and pushed the limits of existing technology to provide a fast, accurate and easy-to-use search service that can be accessed from anywhere. To fully understand Google, it's helpful to understand all the ways in which the company has helped to redefine how individuals, businesses and technologists view the Internet.

TEN THINGS GOOGLE HAS FOUND TO BE TRUE

1. Focus on the user and everything else will follow

From its inception, Google has focused on providing the best user experience possible. While many companies claim to put their customers first, few are able to resist the temptation to make small sacrifices to increase shareholder value. Google has steadfastly refused to make any change that does not benefit the users who come to the site:

- The interface is clear and simple.
- Pages load instantly.
- Placement in search results is never sold to anyone.
- Advertising on the site must offer relevant content and not be a distraction.

By always placing the interests of the user first, Google has built the most loyal audience on the web. And that growth has come not through TV ad campaigns, but through word of mouth from one satisfied user to another.

2. It's best to do one thing really, really well

Google does search. With one of the world's largest research groups focused exclusively on solving search problems, we know what we do well and how we could do it better. Through continued iteration on difficult problems, we've been able to solve complex issues and provide continuous improvements to a service already considered the best on the web at making finding information a fast and seamless experience for millions of users. Our dedication to improving search has also allowed us to apply what we've learned to new products including Google Mail, Google Desktop and Google Maps. As we continue to build new products* while making search better, our hope is to bring the power of search to previously unexplored areas and to help users access and use even more of the ever-expanding information in their lives.

3. Fast is better than slow

Google believes in instant satisfaction. You want answers and you want them right now. Who are we to argue? Google may be the only company in the world whose stated goal is to have users leave its website as quickly as possible. By fanatically fixating on shaving every excess bit and byte from our pages and increasing the efficiency of our serving environment, Google has broken its own speed records time and again. Others assumed large servers were the fastest way to handle massive amounts of data. Google found networked PCs to be faster. Where others accepted apparent speed limits imposed by search algorithms, Google wrote new algorithms that proved there were no limits. And Google continues to work on making it all go even faster.

4. Democracy on the web works

Google works because it relies on the millions of individuals posting websites to determine which other sites offer content of value. Instead of relying on a group of editors or solely on the frequency with which certain terms appear, Google ranks every web page using a breakthrough technique called PageRank™. PageRank evaluates all of the sites linking to a web page and assigns them a value, based in part on the sites linking to them. By analysing the full structure of the web, Google is able to determine which sites have been "voted" the best sources of information by those most interested in the information they offer. This technique actually improves as the web gets bigger, as each new site is another point of information and another vote to be counted.

5. You don't need to be at your desk to need an answer

The world is increasingly mobile and unwilling to be constrained to a fixed location. Whether it's through their PDAs, their wireless phones or even their cars, people want information to come to them. Google's innovations in this area include Google Number Search, which reduces the number of keypad strokes required to find data from a web-enabled mobile phone and an on-the-fly translation system that converts pages written in HTML to a format that can be read by phone browsers. This system opens up billions of pages for viewing from devices that would otherwise not be able to display them including Palm PDAs and Japanese i-mode, J-Sky and EZWeb devices. Wherever search is likely to help users obtain the information they seek, Google is pioneering new technologies and offering new solutions.

6. You can make money without doing evil

Google is a business. The revenue the company generates is derived from offering its <u>search technology</u> to companies and from the sale of <u>advertising</u> displayed on Google and on other sites across the web. However, you may have never seen an ad on Google. That's because Google does not allow ads to be displayed on our results pages unless they're relevant to the results page on which they're shown. So, only certain searches produce sponsored links above or to the right of the results. Google firmly believes that ads can provide useful information if, and only if, they are relevant to what you wish to find.

Google has also proven that advertising can be effective without being flashy. Google does not accept pop-up advertising, which interferes with your ability to see the content you've requested. We've found that text ads (<u>AdWords</u>) that are relevant to the person reading them draw much higher click-through rates than ads appearing randomly. Google's maximisation group works with advertisers to improve click-through rates over the life of a campaign, because high click-through rates are an indication that ads are relevant to a user's interests. Any advertiser, no matter how small or how large, can take advantage of this highly targeted medium, whether through our self-service advertising program that puts ads online within minutes or with the assistance of a Google advertising representative.

Advertising on Google is always clearly identified as a "Sponsored Link." It is a core value for Google that there is no compromise on the integrity of our results. We never manipulate rankings to put our partners higher in our search results. No one can buy better PageRank. Our users trust Google's objectivity and no short-term gain could ever justify breaching that trust.

Thousands of advertisers use our Google AdWords program to promote their products; we believe AdWords is the largest program of its kind. In addition, thousands of web site managers take advantage of our Google AdSense program to deliver ads relevant to the content on their sites, improving their ability to generate revenue and enhancing the experience for their users.

7. There's always more information out there

Once Google had indexed more of the HTML pages on the Internet than any other search service, our engineers turned their attention to information that was not as readily accessible. Sometimes it was just a matter of integrating new databases, such as adding a phone number and address lookup and a business directory. Other efforts required a bit more creativity, like adding the ability to search billions of images and a way to view pages that were originally created as PDF files. The popularity of PDF results led us to expand the list of file types searched to include documents produced in a dozen formats such as Microsoft Word, Excel and PowerPoint. For wireless users, Google developed a unique way to translate HTML formatted files into a format that could be read by mobile devices. The list is not likely to end there as Google's researchers continue looking into ways to bring all the world's information to users looking for answers.

8. The need for information crosses all borders

Although Google's headquarters is in California, our mission is to facilitate access to information for the entire world, so we have offices around the globe. To achieve this, we maintain dozens of Internet domains and serve more than half of our results to users living outside the United States. Google search results can be restricted to pages written in more than 35 languages according to a user's preference. We also offer a translation feature to make content available to users regardless of their native tongue and for those who prefer not to search in English, Google's interface can be customised into more than 100 languages. To accelerate the addition of new languages, Google offers volunteers the opportunity to help in the translation through an automated tool available on the Google.com website. This process has greatly improved both the variety and quality of service we're able to offer users in the most far-flung corners of the globe.

9. You can be serious without a suit

Google's founders have often stated that the company is not serious about anything but search. They built a company around the idea that work should be challenging and the challenge should be fun. To achieve this, Google's culture is unlike any in corporate America, and it's not because of the lava lamps and large rubber balls everywhere, or the fact that the company's chef used to cook for the Grateful Dead. In the same way Google puts users first when it comes to our online service, Google Inc. puts employees first when it comes to daily life in our Googleplex headquarters. There is an emphasis on team achievements and pride in individual accomplishments that contribute to the company's overall success. Ideas are traded, tested and put into practice with an enthusiasm that can make you dizzy. Meetings that would take hours elsewhere are frequently little more than a conversation in the lunch queue and not many walls separate those who write the code from those who write the cheques. This highly communicative environment fosters a productivity and camaraderie fuelled by the realisation that millions of people rely on Google results. Give the proper tools to a group of people who like to make a difference, and they will.

10. Great Just Isn't Good Enough

Always deliver more than expected. Google does not accept being the best as an endpoint, but a starting point. Through innovation and iteration, Google takes something that works well and improves upon it in unexpected ways. Search works well for correctly spelt words, but what about typos? One engineer saw a need and created a spell checker that seems to read a user's mind. It takes too long to search from a WAP phone? Our wireless group developed Google Number Search to reduce entries from three keystrokes per letter to one. With a user base in the millions, Google is able to identify areas of conflict quickly and smooth them out. Google's distinguishing feature, however, is anticipating needs not yet articulated by our global audience, then meeting them with products and services that set new standards. This constant dissatisfaction with the way things are is ultimately the driving force behind the world's best search engine.

*Full-disclosure update: When we first wrote these "10 things" four years ago, we included the phrase "Google does not do horoscopes, financial advice or chat." Over time we've expanded our view of the range of services we can offer — web search, for instance, isn't the only way for people to access or use information — and products that then seemed unlikely are now key aspects of our portfolio. This doesn't mean we've changed our core mission; just that the farther we travel toward achieving it, the more those fuzzy objects on the horizon come into sharper focus (to be replaced, of course, by more fuzzy objects).

Exhibit 4 – Selected Google Acquisitions

Year	Month	Acquisition(s)
2001	February	Deja.com's Usenet Discussion Service
	September	Outride
2003	February	Pyra Labs
	April	Applied Semantics, Neotonic Software
	September	Kaltix Corporation
	October	Sprinks, Genius Labs
2004	May	Ignite Logic
	June	Baidu
	July	Picasa
	September	ZipDash
	October	Where2, Keyhole Incorporated
2005	March	Urchin Software Corporation
	May	Dodgeball
	July	Reqwireless, Current Communications Group
	August	Android
	November	Skia, Akwan Information Technologies
	December	AOL, Phatbits, allPAY GmbH, brunet GmbH
2006	January	dMarc Broadcasting
	February	Measure Map
	March	Upstartle, @Last Software, Writely
	April	Orion
	June	2 Web Technologies
	August	Neven Vision

	October	YouTube, JotSpot
	December	Endoxon
2007	January	Xunlei
	February	Adscape
	March	Trendalyzer
	April	Tonic Systems, Marratech, DoubleClick
	May	GreenBorder
	June	Panoramio, Feedburner, PeakStream, Zenter
	July	Postini, GrandCentral Communications, Image America
	September	Zingku
	October	Jaiku
2008	July	Omnisio
	September	TNC (Tatter and Company)

Exhibit 5 – "An Owner's Manual" for Google's Shareholders[47]

INTRODUCTION

Google is not a conventional company. We do not intend to become one. Throughout Google's evolution as a privately held company, we have managed Google differently. We have also emphasized an atmosphere of creativity and challenge, which has helped us provide unbiased, accurate and free access to information for those who rely on us around the world.

Now the time has come for the company to move to public ownership. This change will bring important benefits for our employees, for our present and future shareholders, for our customers, and most of all for Google users. But the standard structure of public ownership may jeopardize the independence and focused objectivity that have been most important in Google's past success and that we consider most fundamental for its future. Therefore, we have implemented a corporate structure that is designed to protect Google's ability to innovate and retain its most distinctive characteristics. We are confident that, in the long run, this will benefit Google and its shareholders, old and new. We want to clearly explain our plans and the reasoning and values behind them. We are delighted you are considering an investment in Google and are reading this letter.

Sergey and I intend to write you a letter like this one every year in our annual report. We'll take turns writing the letter so you'll hear directly from each of us. We ask that you read this letter in conjunction with the rest of this prospectus.

---

[47] "An Owner's Manual" for Google's Shareholders - http://investor.google.com/ipo_letter.html Much of this was inspired by Warren Buffett's essays in his annual reports and his "An Owner's Manual" to Berkshire Hathaway shareholders.

SERVING END USERS

Sergey and I founded Google because we believed we could provide an important service to the world – instantly delivering relevant information on virtually any topic. Serving our end users is at the heart of what we do and remains our number one priority.

Our goal is to develop services that significantly improve the lives of as many people as possible. In pursuing this goal, we may do things that we believe have a positive impact on the world, even if the near term financial returns are not obvious. For example, we make our services as widely available as we can by supporting over 90 languages and by providing most services for free. Advertising is our principal source of revenue, and the ads we provide are relevant and useful rather than intrusive and annoying. We strive to provide users with great commercial information.

We are proud of the products we have built, and we hope that those we create in the future will have an even greater positive impact on the world.

LONG TERM FOCUS

As a private company, we have concentrated on the long term, and this has served us well. As a public company, we will do the same. In our opinion, outside pressures too often tempt companies to sacrifice long term opportunities to meet quarterly market expectations. Sometimes this pressure has caused companies to manipulate financial results in order to "make their quarter." In Warren Buffett's words, "We won't 'smooth' quarterly or annual results: If earnings figures are lumpy when they reach headquarters, they will be lumpy when they reach you."

If opportunities arise that might cause us to sacrifice short term results but are in the best long term interest of our shareholders, *we will take those opportunities*. We will have the fortitude to do this. We would request that our shareholders take the long term view.

You might ask how long is long term? Usually we expect projects to have some realized benefit or progress within a year or two. But, we are trying to look forward as far as we can. Despite the quickly changing business and technology landscape, we try to look at three to five year scenarios in order to decide what to do now. We try to optimize total benefit over these multi-year scenarios. While we are strong advocates of this strategy, it is difficult to make good multi-year predictions in technology.

Many companies are under pressure to keep their earnings in line with analysts' forecasts. Therefore, they often accept smaller, predictable earnings rather than larger and less predictable returns. Sergey and I feel this is harmful, and we intend to steer in the opposite direction.

Google has had adequate cash to fund our business and has generated additional cash through operations. This gives us the flexibility to weather costs, benefit from opportunities and optimize our long term earnings. For example, in our ads system we make many improvements that affect revenue in both directions. These are in areas like end user relevance and satisfaction, advertiser satisfaction, partner needs and targeting technology. We release improvements immediately rather than delaying them, even though delay might give "smoother" financial results. You have our commitment to execute quickly to achieve long term value rather than making the quarters more predictable.

Our long term focus does have risks. Markets may have trouble evaluating long term value, thus potentially reducing the value of our company. Our long term focus may simply be the wrong business strategy. Competitors may be rewarded for short term tactics and grow stronger as a result. As potential investors, you should consider the risks around our long term focus.

We will make business decisions with the long term welfare of our company and shareholders in mind and not based on accounting considerations.

Although we may discuss long term trends in our business, we do not plan to give earnings guidance in the traditional sense. We are not able to predict our business within a narrow range for each quarter. We recognize that our duty is to advance our shareholders' interests, and we believe that artificially creating short term target numbers serves our shareholders poorly. We would prefer not to be asked to make such predictions, and if asked we will respectfully decline. A management team distracted by a series of short term targets is as pointless as a dieter stepping on a scale every half hour.

RISK VS REWARD IN THE LONG RUN

Our business environment changes rapidly and needs long term investment. We will not hesitate to place major bets on promising new opportunities.

We will not shy away from high-risk, high-reward projects because of short term earnings pressure. Some of our past bets have gone extraordinarily well, and others have not. Because we recognize the pursuit of such projects as the key to our long term success, we will continue to seek them out. For example, we would fund projects that have a 10% chance of earning a billion dollars over the long term. Do not be surprised if we place smaller bets in areas that seem very speculative or even strange when compared to our current businesses. Although we cannot quantify the specific level of risk we will undertake, as the ratio of reward to risk increases, we will accept projects further outside our current businesses, especially when the initial investment is small relative to the level of investment in our current businesses.

We encourage our employees, in addition to their regular projects, to spend 20% of their time working on what they think will most benefit Google. This empowers them to be more creative and innovative. Many of our significant advances have happened in this manner. For example, AdSense for content and Google News were both prototyped in "20% time". Most risky projects fizzle, often teaching us something. Others succeed and become attractive businesses.

As we seek to maximize value in the long term, we may have quarter-to-quarter volatility as we realize losses on some new projects and gains on others. We would love to better quantify our level of risk and reward for you going forward, but that is very difficult. Even though we are excited about risky projects, we expect to devote the vast majority of our resources to improvements to our main businesses (currently search and advertising). Most employees naturally gravitate toward incremental improvements in core areas so this tends to happen naturally.

EXECUTIVE ROLES

We run Google as a triumvirate. Sergey and I have worked closely together for the last eight years, five at Google. Eric, our CEO, joined Google three years ago. The three of us run the company collaboratively with Sergey and me as Presidents. The structure is unconventional, but we have worked successfully in this way.

To facilitate timely decisions, Eric, Sergey and I meet daily to update each other on the business and to focus our collaborative thinking on the most important and immediate issues. Decisions are often made by one of us, with the others being briefed later. This works because we have tremendous trust and respect for each other and we generally think alike. Because of our intense long term working relationship, we can often predict differences of opinion among the three of us. We know that when we disagree, the correct decision is far from obvious. For important decisions, we discuss the issue with a larger team appropriate to the task. Differences are resolved through discussion and analysis and by reaching consensus. Eric, Sergey and I run the company without any significant internal conflict, but with healthy debate. As different topics come up, we often delegate decision-making responsibility to one of us.

We hired Eric as a more experienced complement to Sergey and me to help us run the business. Eric was CTO of Sun Microsystems. He was also CEO of Novell and has a Ph.D. in computer science, a very unusual and important combination for Google given our scientific and technical culture. This partnership among the three of us has worked very well and we expect it to continue. The shared judgments and extra energy available from all three of us has significantly benefited Google.

Eric has the legal responsibilities of the CEO and focuses on management of our vice presidents and the sales organization. Sergey focuses on engineering and business deals. I focus on engineering and product management. All three of us devote considerable time to overall management of the company and other fluctuating needs. We also have a distinguished board of directors to oversee the management of Google. We have a talented executive staff that manages day-to-day operations in areas such as finance, sales, engineering, human resources, public relations, legal and product management. We are extremely fortunate to have talented management that has grown the company to where it is today – they operate the company and deserve the credit.

CORPORATE STRUCTURE

We are creating a corporate structure that is designed for stability over long time horizons. By investing in Google, you are placing an unusual long term bet on the team, especially Sergey and me, and on our innovative approach.

We want Google to become an important and significant institution. That takes time, stability and independence. We bridge the media and technology industries, both of which have experienced considerable consolidation and attempted hostile takeovers.

In the transition to public ownership, we have set up a corporate structure that will make it harder for outside parties to take over or influence Google. This structure will also make it easier for our management team to follow the long term, innovative approach emphasized earlier. This structure, called a dual class voting structure, is described elsewhere in this prospectus. The Class A common stock we are offering has one vote per share, while the Class B common stock held by many current shareholders has 10 votes per share.

The main effect of this structure is likely to leave our team, especially Sergey and me, with increasingly significant control over the company's decisions and fate, as Google shares change hands. After the IPO, Sergey, Eric and I will control 37.6% of the voting power of Google, and the executive management team and directors as a group will control 61.4% of the voting power. New investors will fully share in Google's long term economic future but will have little ability to influence its strategic decisions through their voting rights.

While this structure is unusual for technology companies, similar structures are common in the media business and have had a profound importance there. The New York Times Company, The Washington Post Company and Dow Jones, the publisher of *The Wall Street Journal*, all have similar dual class ownership structures. Media observers have pointed out that dual class ownership has allowed these companies to concentrate on their core, long term interest in serious news coverage, despite fluctuations in quarterly results. Berkshire Hathaway has implemented a dual class structure for similar reasons. From the point of view of long term success in advancing a company's core values, we believe this structure has clearly been an advantage.

Some academic studies have shown that from a purely economic point of view, dual class structures have not harmed the share price of companies. Other studies have concluded that dual class structures have negatively affected share prices, and we cannot assure you that this will not be the case with Google. The shares of each of our classes have identical economic rights and differ only as to voting rights.

Google has prospered as a private company. We believe a dual class voting structure will enable Google, as a public company, to retain many of the positive aspects of being private. We understand some investors do not favor dual class structures. Some may believe that our dual class structure will give us the ability to take actions that benefit us, but not Google's shareholders as a whole. We have considered this point of view carefully, and we and the board have not made our decision lightly. We are convinced that everyone associated with Google – including new investors – will benefit from this structure. However, you should be aware that Google and its shareholders may not realize these intended benefits.

In addition, we have recently expanded our board of directors to include three additional members. John Hennessy is the President of Stanford and has a Doctoral degree in computer science. Art Levinson is CEO of Genentech and has a Ph.D. in biochemistry. Paul Otellini is President and COO of Intel. We could not be more excited about the caliber and experience of these directors.

We believe we have a world class management team impassioned by Google's mission and responsible for Google's success. We believe the stability afforded by the dual class structure will enable us to retain our unique culture and continue to attract and retain talented people who are Google's life blood. Our colleagues will be able to trust that they themselves and their labors of hard work, love and creativity will be well cared for by a company focused on stability and the long term.

As an investor, you are placing a potentially risky long term bet on the team, especially Sergey and me. The two of us, Eric and the rest of the management team recognize that our individual and collective interests are deeply aligned with those of the new investors who choose to support Google. Sergey and I are committed to Google for the long term. The broader Google team has also demonstrated an extraordinary commitment to our long term success. With continued hard work and good fortune, this commitment will last and flourish.

When Sergey and I founded Google, we hoped, but did not expect, it would reach its current size and influence. Our intense and enduring interest was to objectively help people find information efficiently. We also believed that searching and organizing all the world's information was an unusually important task that should be carried out by a company that is trustworthy and interested in the public good. We believe a well functioning society should have abundant, free and unbiased access to high quality information. Google therefore has a responsibility to the world. The dual class structure helps ensure that this responsibility is met. We believe that fulfilling this responsibility will deliver increased value to our shareholders.

IPO PRICING AND ALLOCATION

It is important to us to have a fair process for our IPO that is inclusive of both small and large investors. It is also crucial that we achieve a good outcome for Google and its current shareholders. This has led us to pursue an auction-based IPO for our entire offering. Our goal is to have a share price that reflects an efficient market valuation of Google that moves rationally based on changes in our business and the stock market. (The auction process is discussed in more detail elsewhere in this prospectus.)

Many companies going public have suffered from unreasonable speculation, small initial share float, and stock price volatility that hurt them and their investors in the long run. We believe that our auction-based IPO will minimize these problems, though there is no guarantee that it will.

An auction is an unusual process for an IPO in the United States. Our experience with auction-based advertising systems has been helpful in the auction design process for the IPO. As in the stock market, if people bid for more shares than are available and bid at high prices, the IPO price will be higher. Of course, the IPO price will be lower if there are not enough bidders or if people bid lower prices. This is a simplification, but it captures the basic issues. Our goal is to have the price of our shares at the IPO and in the aftermarket reflect an efficient market price – in other words, a price set by rational and informed buyers and sellers. We seek to achieve a relatively stable price in the days following the IPO and that buyers and sellers receive an efficient market price at the IPO. We will try to achieve this outcome, but of course may not be successful. Our goal of achieving a relatively stable market price may result in Google determining with our underwriters to set the initial public offering price below the auction clearing price.

We are working to create a sufficient supply of shares to meet investor demand at IPO time and after. We are encouraging current shareholders to consider selling some of their shares as part of the offering. These shares will supplement the shares the company sells to provide more supply for investors and hopefully provide a more stable price. Sergey and I, among others, are currently planning to sell a fraction of our shares in the IPO. The more shares current shareholders sell, the more likely it is that they believe the price is not unfairly low. The supply of shares available will likely have an effect on the clearing price of the auction. Since the number of shares being sold is likely to be larger at a high price and smaller at a lower price, investors will likely want to consider the scope of current shareholder participation in the IPO. We may communicate from time to time that we are sellers rather than buyers at certain prices.

While we have designed our IPO to be inclusive for both small and large investors, for a variety of reasons described in "Auction Process" not all interested investors will be able to receive an allocation of shares in our IPO.

We would like you to invest for the long term, and you should not expect to sell Google shares for a profit shortly after Google's IPO. We encourage investors not to invest in Google at IPO or for some time after, if they believe the price is not sustainable over the long term. Even in the long term, the trading price of Google's stock may decline.

We intend to take steps to help ensure shareholders are well informed. We encourage you to read this prospectus, especially the Risk Factors section. We think that short term speculation without paying attention to price is likely to lose you money, especially with our auction structure. In particular, we caution you that investing in Google through our auction could be followed by a significant decline in the value of your investment after the IPO.

GOOGLERS

Our employees, who have named themselves Googlers, are everything. Google is organized around the ability to attract and leverage the talent of exceptional technologists and business people. We have been lucky to recruit many creative, principled and hard working stars. We hope to recruit many more in the future. We will reward and treat them well.

We provide many unusual benefits for our employees, including meals free of charge, doctors and washing machines. We are careful to consider the long term advantages to the company of these benefits. Expect us to add benefits rather than pare them down over time. We believe it is easy to be penny wise and pound foolish with respect to benefits that can save employees considerable time and improve their health and productivity.

The significant employee ownership of Google has made us what we are today. Because of our employee talent, Google is doing exciting work in nearly every area of computer science. We are in a very competitive industry where the quality of our product is paramount. Talented people are attracted to Google because we empower them to change the world; Google has large computational resources and distribution that enables individuals to make a difference. Our main benefit is a workplace with important projects, where employees can contribute and grow. We are focused on providing an environment where talented, hard working people are rewarded for their contributions to Google and for making the world a better place.

DON'T BE EVIL

Don't be evil. We believe strongly that in the long term, we will be better served — as shareholders and in all other ways — by a company that does good things for the world even if we forego some short term gains. This is an important aspect of our culture and is broadly shared within the company.

Google users trust our systems to help them with important decisions: medical, financial and many others. Our search results are the best we know how to produce. They are unbiased and objective, and we do not accept payment for them or for inclusion or more frequent updating. We also display advertising, which we work hard to make relevant, and we label it clearly. This is similar to a well-run newspaper, where the advertisements are clear and the articles are not influenced by the advertisers' payments. We believe it is important for everyone to have access to the best information and research, not only to the information people pay for you to see.

MAKING THE WORLD A BETTER PLACE

We aspire to make Google an institution that makes the world a better place. In pursuing this goal, we will always be mindful of our responsibilities to our shareholders, employees, customers and business partners. With our products, Google connects people and information all around the world for free. We are adding other powerful services such as Gmail, which provides an efficient one gigabyte Gmail account for free. We know that some people have raised privacy concerns, primarily over Gmail's targeted ads, which could lead to negative perceptions about Google. However, we believe Gmail protects a user's privacy. By releasing services, such as Gmail, for free, we hope to help bridge the digital divide. AdWords connects users and advertisers efficiently, helping both. AdSense helps fund a huge variety of online web sites and enables authors who could not otherwise publish. Last year we created Google Grants – a growing program in which hundreds of non-profits addressing issues, including the environment, poverty and human rights, receive free advertising. And now, we are in the process of establishing the Google Foundation. We intend to contribute significant resources to the foundation, including employee time and approximately 1% of Google's equity and profits in some form. We hope some day this institution may eclipse Google itself in terms of overall world impact by ambitiously applying innovation and significant resources to the largest of the world's problems.

SUMMARY AND CONCLUSION

Google is not a conventional company. Eric, Sergey and I intend to operate Google differently, applying the values it has developed as a private company to its future as a public company. Our mission and business description are available in the rest of this prospectus; we encourage you to carefully read this information. We will optimize for the long term rather than trying to produce smooth earnings for each quarter. We will support selected high-risk, high-reward projects and manage our portfolio of projects. We will run the company collaboratively with Eric, our CEO, as a team of three. We are conscious of our duty as fiduciaries for our shareholders, and we will fulfil those responsibilities. We will continue to strive to attract creative, committed new employees, and we will welcome support from new shareholders. We will live up to our "don't be evil" principle by keeping user trust and not accepting payment for search results. We have a dual class structure that is biased toward stability and independence and that requires investors to bet on the team, especially Sergey and me.

In this letter we have talked about our IPO auction method and our desire for stability and access for all investors. We have discussed our goal to have investors who invest for the long term. Finally, we have discussed our desire to create an ideal working environment that will ultimately drive the success of Google by retaining and attracting talented Googlers.

We have tried hard to anticipate your questions. It will be difficult for us to respond to them given legal constraints during our offering process. We look forward to a long and hopefully prosperous relationship with you, our new investors. We wrote this letter to help you understand our company.

We have a strong commitment to our users worldwide, their communities, the web sites in our network, our advertisers, our investors, and of course our employees. Sergey and I, and the team will do our best to make Google a long term success and the world a better place.

Larry Page

Larry Page

Sergey Brin

Sergey Brin

Exhibit 6 – Selected Search Statistics

Top 10 Search Providers for August 2008 (US)[48]

Provider	Searches (Thousands)	Year On Year Growth	Share of Searches
Google Search	4,331,153	3.1%	60.0%
Yahoo! Search	1,304,889	– 16.5%	18.1%
MSN/Windows Live Search	770,592	– 23.8%	10.7%
AOL Search	376,331	– 13.5%	5.2%
Ask.com	143,231	4.7%	2.0%
Comcast Search	45,438	30.9%	0.6%
My Web Search	38,550	– 46.3%	0.5%
AT&T Worldnet Search	30,272	203.8%	0.4%
NexTag Search	17,901	– 20.6%	0.2%
Dogpile.com	15,418	– 27.8%	0.2%

Source: Nielsen Online, MegaView Search; The Nielsen Company (2009) Available at:
http://blog.nielsen.com/nielsenwire/online_mobile/top-10-search-providers-for-april-2009-us/,
Accessed on 2 June 2009.

US Core Search Share 2008[49]

(% of market)	Jan	Feb	Mar	Apr	May	June	July	Aug	Sep	Oct	Nov	Dec
Google Search	58.5	59.2	59.8	61.6	61.8	61.5	61.9	63.3	62.9	63.1	63.5	63.5
Yahoo! Search	22.2	21.6	21.3	20.4	20.6	20.9	20.5	19.7	20.2	20.5	20.4	20.5
AOL Search	4.9	4.9	4.8	4.6	4.5	4.1	4.2	4.3	4.1	3.7	3.8	3.8
MSN/ Windows Live Search	9.8	9.6	9.4	9.1	8.5	9.2	8.9	8.4	8.5	8.5	8.3	8.3
Ask.com	4.5	4.6	4.7	4.3	4.5	4.3	4.5	4.3	4.3	4.2	4	3.9

Source: comScore qSearch

Exhibit 7 – Selected Google Product Profiles[50]

Google.com – Search and Personalization

- *Google Web Search* – easy access to billions of web pages with Advanced Search Functionality, Web Page Translation, Integrated Tools, Search by Number, Cached Links, Movie, Music and Weather Information, and News, Finance, Maps, Image, Video, Book, Blogs and Groups Information.

---

[48] Nielsen Online, MegaView Search - http://blog.nielsen.com/nielsenwire/online_mobile/top-10-search-providers-for-april-2009-us/

[49] ComScore, Various Press Releases - http://www.comscore.com/Press_Events/Press_Releases

[50] Google Annual Report 2008, Pages 2-14 - http://investor.google.com/pdf/2008_google_annual_report.pdf

- *Google Image Search* – searchable index of images found across the web.
- *Google Book Search* – allows users to search the full text of a library-sized collection of books to discover books of interest and to learn where to buy or borrow them.
- *Google Scholar* – a simple way to do a broad search for relevant scholarly literature including peer-reviewed papers, theses, books, abstracts, and articles.
- *Google Finance* – a simple user interface to navigate complex financial information in an intuitive manner, including linking together different data sources, such as correlating stock price movements to news events.
- *Google News* – information gathered from thousands of news sources worldwide and presents news stories in a searchable format within minutes of their publication on the web.
- *Google Video* – allows users to upload, find, view and share video content worldwide.
- *Google Blog Search* – enables users to search the blogging universe more effectively and find out users' opinions on a wide variety of subjects.
- *iGoogle and Personalized Search* – iGoogle connects users to the information that is most useful and important to them in an easy-to-use and customizable format. iGoogle includes Personalized Search, which gives users better search results based on what they have searched for in the past, making it easier to quickly find the information that is more relevant to them.
- *Google Product Search* – helps users find and compare products from online stores across the web and directs users to where they can buy these products.
- *Google Custom Search* – allows communities of users familiar with particular topics to build customised search engines. These customised search engines allow the communities to help improve the quality of search results by labelling and annotating relevant web pages or by creating specialised, subscribed links for users to get more detailed information about a particular topic.
- *Google Base* – lets content owners submit content that they want to share on Google web sites.
- *Google Webmaster Tools* – provides information to webmasters to help them enhance their understanding of how their web sites interact with the Google search engine.

Applications

- *Google Docs* – application to create, view and edit documents, spreadsheets, and presentations from anywhere using a browser.
- *Google Calendar* – a free online shareable calendar service.
- *Gmail* – free webmail service with built-in Google search technology.
- *Google Groups* – a free service that helps groups of people connect to information and people that have interest in them.
- *Google Reader* – a free service that lets users subscribe to feeds and receive updates from multiple web sites in a single interface.
- *Orkut* – enables users to search and connect to other users through networks of trusted friends.
- *Blogger* – a Web-based publishing tool that lets people publish to the web instantly using weblogs, or "blogs."

- *Google Sites* – allows users to easily create, update and publish content online without technical expertise, with control over who can see and update the site.
- *YouTube* – an online community that lets users worldwide upload, share, watch, rate, and comment on videos, from user generated, niche professional, to premium videos.

Client

- *Google Toolbar* – a free application that adds a Google search box to web browsers (Internet Explorer and Firefox).
- *Google Chrome* – an open-source browser.
- *Google Pack* – a free collection of safe, useful software programs from Google and other companies including programs that help users browse the web faster, remove spyware and viruses.
- *Picasa* – a free service that allows users to view, manage and share their photos.
- *Google Desktop* – lets people perform a full-text search on the contents of their own computer, including email, files, instant messenger chats and web browser history.

Google GEO – Maps, Earth and Local

- *Google Earth* – lets users see and explore the world and beyond from their desktop. Users can fly virtually to a specific location and learn about that area through detailed satellite and aerial images, 3D topography, street maps and millions of data points describing the location of businesses, schools, parks and other points of interest around the globe. Google Earth includes Sky, an astronomical imagery library with images of over 100 million stars and 200 million galaxies, and Ocean, with a detailed bathymetric map of the earth's ocean floors.
- *Google Maps* – helps people navigate map information. Users can look up addresses, search for businesses, and get point-to-point driving directions, all plotted on an interactive street map or on satellite imagery. Google Maps includes StreetView, 360-degree street-level imagery available in several regions around the world, and Google Transit, which provides up-to-date information on local transit options in many cities.
- *Google Sketchup and Sketchup Pro* – a free tool that enables users to model buildings in 3D, and can be used as a tool for populating Google Earth with architectural content. The Pro version of this tool is sold to professional designers and includes additional features.

Google Mobile and Android

- *Google Mobile* – lets people search and view both the "mobile Web", consisting of pages created specifically for wireless devices, and the entire Google index.
- *Google Maps for Mobile* – a free Java client application that lets users view maps and satellite imagery, find local businesses and get driving directions on mobile devices.
- *Blogger for Mobile* – users can take pictures with their camera phones and then post their pictures and text comments to their blog using MMS or email.
- *Google Gmail, News and Personalised Home for Mobile* – Google services available as mobile applications.

- *GOOG-411* – a free, speech-enabled application allowing users to call 1-800-GOOG-411 to search for businesses by name or category.
- *Android* – a free, open-source mobile software platform which allows developers to create applications for mobile devices and for handset manufacturers to install.
- *Search by Voice* – lets users do a Google web search just by saying what they are looking for. Search results are formatted to fit phone screens.

Google Checkout

Google Checkout is a service for users, advertisers and participating merchants that is intended to make online shopping faster, more convenient and more secure by providing a single login for buying online and helping users find convenient and secure places to shop when they search.

For merchants, Google Checkout is integrated with AdWords to help advertisers attract more leads, convert more leads to sales and process sales. Merchants who use Google Checkout are charged 2% of the transaction amount plus $0.20 per transaction to the extent these transactions exceed 10 times the amount they spend on AdWords advertising.

Google Labs

Google Labs is Google's test bed for their engineers and adventurous Google users. Current Google Labs examples include: *Picasa for Mac,* a software that allows Mac users to organise, edit, create and share photos; *In Quotes,* a feature that allows users to find quotes from stories linked to Google News; and *Google Audio Indexing,* a new technology that allow users to find spoken words inside videos and jump to the right portion of the video where these words are spoken.

Google AdWords

Google AdWords is an auction-based advertising program that lets advertisers deliver relevant ads targeted to search queries or web content across Google sites and through the web sites of the Google Network. This is the network of online and offline third parties that use Google advertising programs to deliver relevant ads with their search results and content. The Google Network is also increasingly encompassing different forms of online and offline media as well, including content providers who use advertising programs to deliver ads in online video, television and radio broadcasts. AdWords is accessible to advertisers in 41 different interface languages.

Google AdSense

Google AdSense enables web sites that are part of the Google Network to deliver AdWords ads that are relevant to the search results or content on their pages. It also allows offline media companies, such as television and radio stations, to deliver ads and audio ads to the content they provide. Google share most of the revenue generated from ads shown by a Google Network member with that member.

Display Advertising

Display advertising is internet advertising that typically includes static or animated images as well as interactive audio or video media, such as the banner ads you see on the tops or sides of many popular web sites. Google's acquisition of DoubleClick provides Google with a platform for delivering display advertising. DoubleClick also provides services related to the delivery of display advertising, including media planning, buying, implementation and measurement tools for advertisers and agencies and forecasting and reporting tools for publishers.

Google Enterprise

Google provides a range of software and services for use by educational and business organisations including Google Apps, Google Mini, and Google Search Appliance.

Exhibit 8 – Selected Google Executive Management Profiles[51]

Eric Schmidt: Chairman of the Board and Chief Executive Officer

Google founders Larry Page and Sergey Brin recruited Eric Schmidt from Novell, where he led that company's strategic planning, management and technology development as chairman and CEO. Since coming to Google in 2001, Eric has focused on building the corporate infrastructure needed to maintain Google's rapid growth as a company and on ensuring that quality remains high, while product development cycle times are kept to a minimum. Along with Larry and Sergey, Eric shares responsibility for Google's day-to-day operations. Eric's Novell experience culminated a 20-year record of achievement as an Internet strategist, entrepreneur and developer of great technologies. His well-seasoned perspective perfectly complements Google's needs as a young and rapidly growing search engine with a unique corporate culture.

Prior to his appointment at Novell, Eric was Chief Technology Officer and Corporate Executive officer at Sun Microsystems, Inc., where he led the development of Java, Sun's platform-independent programming technology, and defined Sun's Internet software strategy. Before joining Sun in 1983, he was a member of the research staff at the Computer Science Lab at Xerox Palo Alto Research Center (PARC), and held positions at Bell Laboratories and Zilog. Eric has a bachelor's degree in electrical engineering from Princeton University, and a master's and Ph.D. in computer science from the University of California, Berkeley. In 2006, Eric was elected to the National Academy of Engineering, which recognised his work on "the development of strategies for the world's most successful Internet search engine company." Eric was inducted into the American Academy of Arts and Sciences as a Fellow in 2007. He is also chairman of the board of directors for the New America Foundation.

Larry Page: Co-Founder & President, Products

Larry Page was Google's founding CEO and grew the company to more than 200 employees and profitability before moving into his role as President of Products in April 2001. He continues to share responsibility for Google's day-to-day operations with Eric Schmidt and Sergey Brin.

The son of Michigan State University computer science professor Dr. Carl Victor Page, Larry's love of computers began at the age of six. While following in his father's footsteps in academia, he graduated

---

[51] Google Corporate Information - http://www.google.co.uk/corporate/execs.html

with honours from the University of Michigan, where he earned a Bachelor's degree in engineering, with a concentration on computer engineering. During his time in Ann Arbor, Larry built an inkjet printer out of Lego™ bricks.

While in the PhD programme in computer science at Stanford University, Larry met Sergey Brin, and together they developed and ran Google, which began operating in 1998. Larry went on leave from Stanford after earning his Master's degree.

In 2002, Larry was named a World Economic Forum Global Leader for Tomorrow. He is a member of the National Advisory Committee (NAC) of the University of Michigan College of Engineering and, together with co-founder Sergey Brin, Larry was honoured with the Marconi Prize in 2004. He is a trustee on the board of the X PRIZE, and was elected to the National Academy of Engineering in 2004.

Sergey Brin: Co-Founder & President, Technology

Sergey Brin, a native of Moscow, received a Bachelor of Science degree with honours in mathematics and computer science from the University of Maryland at College Park. He is currently on leave from the PhD programme in computer science at Stanford University, where he received his master's degree. Sergey is a recipient of a National Science Foundation Graduate Fellowship as well as an honorary MBA from Instituto de Empresa. It was at Stanford that he met Larry Page and worked on the project that became Google. Together they founded Google Inc. in 1998 and Sergey continues to share responsibility for day-to-day operations with Larry Page and Eric Schmidt.

Sergey's research interests include search engines, information extraction from unstructured sources and data mining of large text collections and scientific data. He has published more than a dozen academic papers, including *Extracting Patterns and Relations from the World Wide Web; Dynamic Data Mining: A New Architecture for Data with High Dimensionality*, which he published with Larry Page; *Scalable Techniques for Mining Casual Structures; Dynamic Itemset Counting and Implication Rules for Market Basket Data;* and *Beyond Market Baskets: Generalising Association Rules to Correlations.*

Sergey has been a featured speaker at several international academic, business and technology forums, including the World Economic Forum and the Technology, Entertainment and Design Conference. He has shared his views on the technology industry and the future of search on CNBC and CNNfn. In 2004, he and Larry Page were named "Persons of the Week" by ABC World News Tonight.

Google Inc. B – Google Ireland Ltd

Theodore Lynn, Louise Gorman and Malcolm Brady

> "Google, Yahoo and Facebook have their European headquarters in Ireland. However, in recent years businesses have complained that labour and utility costs have risen as the economy overheated."[52]

In 2003, Google opened the doors to its EMEA Operations Headquarters in Dublin. Since then, it has become a major employer with over 1,600 people speaking more than 50 different languages and supporting over 25 countries. It has been voted one of Ireland's "Best Companies to Work For" three times in the last five years.[53]

Ireland has been attractive to web technology companies due to appealing tax incentives and access to a high quality and young talent pool. As well as Google, Yahoo, eBay/Paypal, Ask, AOL and Facebook all have key offices in Dublin.[54]

In May 2009, President Barack Obama signalled the beginning of tax reforms by the US Treasury.[55] The proposed tax changes may affect Google's Dublin operations in that US multinationals operating abroad could potentially no longer defer tax on foreign profits. Furthermore, it seemed that the company might no longer be able to claim tax deductions on many foreign expenses, such as interest costs, until they repatriated earnings. In 2008, Google recorded a pre-tax figure of $3,793.7 million in income from subsidiaries abroad and recorded $19.8 million in deferred foreign taxes. The cumulative amount of earnings upon which US income taxes was not provided was approximately $7.7 billion.[56]

At the same time, Ireland is in the midst of a recession, reflecting the wider global economic downturn. Expenditure on infrastructure is threatened and the IT graduate pool is not being

---

[52] Murray Brown, J., "Ireland to lose 1,900 jobs as Dell moves to Poland", *Financial Times*, 8 January 2009

[53] Great Places to Work, http://www.greatplacetowork.com/best/search-results.php?

[54] IDA Ireland, Entertainment and Media - http://www.idaireland.com/business-in-ireland/media-and-entertainment/what/

[55] Remarks made by the President on International Tax Policy Reform – http://www.whitehouse.gov/the_press_office/Remarks-By-The-President-On-International-Tax-Policy-Reform/

[56] Google Annual Report 2008, Page 94 - http://investor.google.com/pdf/2008_google_annual_report.pdf

maintained. After over a decade, the Government is considering the re-introduction of fees at a time when the pool of new graduates in science and technology are in decline.[57]

Many of the conventional technology companies that located in Ireland in 1970s and 1980s are moving their manufacturing operations to lower cost markets such as Eastern Europe and China. Should Google move their EMEA Operations Headquarters? Could they, even if they wanted?

---

[57] "Fees possible as students protest" - http://www.rte.ie/news/2009/0204/fees.html

Exhibit 1 – Comparative Tax Rates[58]

Jurisdiction	Statutory	Surtax	Local	Effective	Branch Tax
Argentina	35	-	-	35	35
Australia	30	-	-	30	30
Austria	25	-	-	25	25
Belgium	33	3	-	33.99	33
Brazil	34	10	-	34	34
Bulgaria	10	-	-	10	10
Canada	19.5	-	9.9-16	32-38.1	19.5/25
Chile	17	-	-	17	17
China	25	-	-	25	25
Colombia	33	-	-	33	33
Cyprus	10	-	-	10	10
Czech Republic	20	-	-	20	20
Denmark	25	-	-	25	25
Ecuador	25	-	-	25	25
Estonia	21	-	-	21	21
Finland	26	-	-	26	26
France	33.33	3.3	-	34.43	33.33
Germany	15	5.5	14/17	30-33	15
Gibraltar	27	-	-	27	27
Greece	25	3	-	25	25
Hong Kong	16.5	-	-	16.5	16.5
Hungary	16	-	0-2	20	16
Iceland	15	-	-	15	15
India	30/40	10	-	33.99/42.23	40
Indonesia	28	-	-	28	28/20
Ireland	12.5	-	-	12.5	12.5
Israel	26	-	-	26	26
Italy	27.5	-	3.9	Varies	27.5
Japan	30	-	Varies	41	30
Kazakhstan	20	-	-	20/30	20/15
Korea (R.O.K.)	22	-	2.2	24.5	22/05/2015
Latvia	15	-	-	15	15
Lithuania	20	-	-	20	20
Luxembourg	21	-	6.75	28.59	21
Malaysia	25	-	-	25	25
Malta	35	-	-	35	35
Mauritius	15	-	-	3	15
Mexico	28	-	-	28	28

---

[58] Deloitte International Tax Source-
http://www.dits.deloitte.com/DomesticRates/domesticRatesMatrix.aspx

Netherlands	25.5	-	-	25.5	25.5
New Zealand	30	-	-	30	30
Norway	28	-	-	28	28
Peru	30	-	-	30	30/4.1
Philippines	30	10	-	30	30/15
Poland	19	-	-	19	19
Portugal	25	-	0-1.5	26.5	25
Romania	16	-	-	16	16
Russia	20	-	17.5	20	20
Singapore	17	-	-	17	17
Slovakia	19	-	-	19	19
Slovenia	21	-	-	21	21
South Africa	28	-	-	34.545	33
Spain	30		0.01-0.75	30	30/18/15
Sweden	26.3	-	-	26.3	26.3
Switzerland	8.5	-	0-18	7.8	8.5
Taiwan	25	10		25	25
Thailand	30	-	-	30	30
Turkey	20	-	-	20	20
Ukraine	25	-	-	25	25
United Kingdom	28	-	-	28	28
United States	35	-	0-12	39.5	35
Uruguay	25	-	-	25	25
Venezuela	15-34	-	0.5-10	15-34	15-34
Vietnam	25	-	-	25	25

Source: Deloitte International Tax Source, 2008

Exhibit 2 – Broadband subscribers per 100 inhabitants in OECD countries (June 2008)[59]

Rank		DSL	Cable	Fibre/LAN	Other	Total	Total subscribers	OECD average
1	Denmark	22.6	9.9	3.6	1.1	37.2	2,021,404	22.6
2	Netherlands	21.8	13.4	0.6	0.0	35.8	5,855,000	22.6
5	Iceland	31.6	0.0	0.6	0.6	32.8	99,883	22.6
3	Norway	23.8	6.9	3.1	0.7	34.5	1,607,750	22.6
4	Switzerland	23.2	9.7	0.4	0.3	33.5	2,533,643	22.6
8	Finland	25.9	4.1	0.0	0.7	30.7	1,616,900	22.6
6	Korea	7.7	10.5	13.8	0.0	32.0	15,474,931	22.6
7	Sweden	19.1	6.2	6.5	0.2	32.0	2,905,000	22.6
9	Luxembourg	25.6	4.2	0.1	0.0	30.0	141,584	22.6
10	Canada	13.0	15.6	0.0	0.4	29.0	9,577,648	22.6
11	United Kingdom	22.4	6.1	0.0	0.1	28.5	17,275,660	22.6
12	Belgium	16.4	11.4	0.0	0.3	28.1	2,962,450	22.6
13	France	26.6	1.4	0.1	0.0	28.0	17,725,000	22.6
14	Germany	25.4	1.9	0.0	0.0	27.4	22,532,000	22.6
15	United States	11.1	13.7	1.0	0.9	26.7	80,071,074	22.6
16	Australia	19.9	4.3	0.0	1.2	25.4	5,368,000	22.6
17	Japan	9.1	3.2	11.3	0.0	23.6	30,107,327	22.6
19	Austria	13.9	7.2	0.1	0.5	21.6	1,792,408	22.6
18	New Zealand	19.5	1.3	0.0	1.0	21.9	914,961	22.6
21	Ireland	15.1	2.4	0.1	2.9	20.6	896,346	22.6
20	Spain	16.5	4.0	0.1	0.2	20.8	9,156,969	22.6
22	Italy	18.5	0.0	0.5	0.1	19.2	11,283,000	22.6

[59] OECD Key ICT Indicators - http://www.oecd.org/dataoecd/21/35/39574709.xls

Rank		DSL	Cable	Fibre/LAN	Other	Total	Total subscribers	OECD average
23	Czech Republic	6.8	3.7	0.7	6.0	17.2	1,769,684	22.6
25	Portugal	9.4	6.3	0.0	0.2	16.0	1,692,306	22.6
24	Hungary	7.9	7.6	0.5	0.9	16.8	1,696,714	22.6
26	Greece	13.5	0.0	0.0	0.0	13.5	1,506,614	22.6
28	Poland	7.2	3.1	0.0	0.1	10.5	3,995,458	22.6
27	Slovak Republic	6.6	1.2	2.1	1.6	11.5	618,871	22.6
29	Turkey	7.7	0.1	0.0	0.0	7.8	5,736,619	22.6
30	Mexico	5.1	1.9	0.0	0.2	7.2	7,604,629	22.6
	OECD	13.6	6.4	2.2	0.4	22.6	266,539,833	22.6

Source: OECD, 2008

SUGGESTED SOLUTIONS

CHAPTER 1 – SUGGESTED SOLUTIONS

Exercise 1.1: Suggested Solution

(**Note:** The discipline of identifying possible actions that will help you towards your goal is part of the process of making the objective real and achievable.)

Did you consider:

- What blockages might impede your ability to take the identified actions? How might these be overcome?
- Who do you know who has run a marathon? What might they tell you?
- Is this a once-off event or perhaps a change of direction in your life? If a significant change is envisaged a bigger and consistent response will be needed.

This is a simple 'brainstorming' exercise to list 10 possible actions you might take – not in any particular order:

- Develop an exercise plan.
- Join a running club.
- Monitor your progress against the plan.
- Get a running mate who will encourage you to remain committed to your plan.
- Have some 'milestones' to work towards with some way of celebrating your success.
- Acquire appropriate running equipment/heart monitor.
- Assess how fit you are and consider the need for a medical check up.
- Review your diet to consider how this might be improved to support your goal.
- Plan for intermediate activities, e.g. half marathons, 10km races, etc. to give you focus.
- Put a chart on your bedroom wall tracking your progress.
- Build a social network to support your plan.
- Consider similar achievements that you have done in the past – what ideas worked? What lessons can you apply here, etc.?

Exercise 1.2: Outline Solution

Direction of the business Aer Lingus's board made a fundamental change in direction to model itself on Ryanair and to move away from being a national carrier/full service operation.

Scope of the business The decision to move to being a low-cost carrier would require Aer Lingus to focus on areas congruent with the low-cost model (heavily discounted fares; no business or first class, except on long-haul; and the closure of freight and catering, which was outsourced for cost reasons). Interestingly, in more recent years Aer Lingus has re-entered the freight activity – it is quite a profitable activity.

Long term The strategic decision to change the scope of activity was a long-term change and would affect the decisions of Aer Lingus in terms of airplane purchases, staff training, divisional expansion or contraction in the long term.

(Competitive) advantage Aer Lingus was now competing as a low-cost carrier (Porter would call this a "cost leader"). This would require a radical examination of Aer Lingus's operating procedures and cost structures to reduce these and enable lower cost fares to be charged. This impacted on such things as contracts, pay rates and the need for more flexible work practices. In the short term Aer Lingus shed surplus staff, and those who remained were on new contracts. One of the challenges for Aer Lingus has been the need to keep adapting to Ryanair's relentless cost cutting!

Resources (or competences) Aer Lingus's traditional competence was as a national carrier ("flying the flag") offering a friendly service to and from Ireland. This competence was no longer relevant, given the onslaught from Ryanair. Some additional competencies would need to be developed which were appropriate to the low-cost carrier model. Aer Lingus has sought to position itself as a low-cost carrier but not to the same extent as Ryanair.

Changing environment The deregulation of the airline industry in Europe was a key change which, in turn, spawned many low-cost carriers, the most successful of these being Ryanair. Ryanair has continued to squeeze its cost base, requiring Aer Lingus and other carriers to compete or lose market share. Customers continue to favour low-cost options for their personal travel. The Internet offered options to reduce costs further. The recent recession has kept the low-cost option as a key preference for customers.

Stakeholder expectations As a state-owned carrier, Aer Lingus is affected by the expectations of its shareholder – the Government – which is affected by pressure from the employees in Aer Lingus. The State was restricted in its ability to bail out Aer Lingus due to competition laws. Semi-state companies are typically heavily unionised with restrictive work practices. Willie Walsh had to use the threat of Aer Lingus going out of business to challenge these expectations. Customers were opting for low-cost carriers. This preference has remained. Bankers would expect that the losses in Aer Lingus would be addressed. Aer Lingus has had to go through a series of restructuring of work practices as a means of challenging its industrial relations practices.

Was the Strategy Successful?

Arguably, the strategy has enabled Aer Lingus to continue in existence – without it, closure was likely (witness Sabena, the Belgian national carrier, or Swiss Air). The segment in which they operate remains dynamic and challenging. Subsequently, Dermot Mannion, as CEO, introduced some new long-haul routes which, given the economic downturn, were not profitable. The current CEO, Christoph Mueller, has had to axe these routes and push through further cost-cutting.

What Challenges Remain?

As the market is changing, Aer Lingus must adapt its business model (and cost base) to:

- Changing economic circumstances (downturn, fuel prices)
- Changing technology

- Different attitudes to flying, including global warming issues
- Changing legislation
- Altering stakeholder perspectives – it is a listed company with Ryanair as a major shareholder, etc.

The future success of Aer Lingus will depend on how well its strategy gains competitive advantage in the ever-changing dynamic market it operates within.

Exercise 1.3: Outline Solution

Corporate level At a corporate level, the decision to be a low-cost carrier determined the long-term direction and scope for the airline. This affects what business Aer Lingus is in. This decision would be made by the Board.

Divisional level Aer Lingus closed down two divisions – catering and freight – which were not seen as key to the low-cost philosophy. (Freight has since been reintroduced.)

Functional Strategies

- The low cost philosophy impacted on the functional strategies of Aer Lingus such as the HR strategy.
- The proposed HR strategy ended up in the media when it was reported that consideration was being given to "counselling out" older staff and the adoption of 'jump suits' work wear for cabin crew.

Exercise 1.4: Suggested Solution

(a) Mission and Objectives (aim to have a clear objective in mind):

- Do I have a mission or set of values that I can use to motivate myself in my training programme?
- Do I have a clear "vision" of what I want to become at the end of this "journey"?
- What objectives am I setting for myself in this challenge?
- Do I have other subsidiary goals (like having "fun" along the way)?
- How can I balance this objective with other challenges?

(b) Environmental Analysis (purpose is to understand the environment in which I operate and the threats and opportunities this poses for my marathon plan):

- Consider my:
    - o Work situation
    - o Study needs

- o Social life and needs
- o Family and other challenges

- How can I fit my plan of running the marathon into these conflicting requirements?

(c) Position Audit (the aim is to assess where I am in terms of my strengths and weaknesses, particularly those related to my objective):

- How fit am I?
- What has been my previous running experience?
- What resources and supports can I draw on?
- What weaknesses (or temptations) might undermine my progress?

(d) Personal Appraisal (matching my strengths/weaknesses to the environment):

- Can I combine my strengths to seize the opportunity, and benefits, presented by running a marathon?
- Can I tackle my weaknesses to do this? Be specific!

(e) Strategic Option Generation:

- There are presumably a number of alternative strategies you might follow:
  - o Train on your own
  - o Join a running club
  - o Hire a personal trainer

(f) Strategic Evaluation and Choice (aim to select a strategy or strategies to enable you to achieve your goal):

- Ultimately, you will choose an approach that best suits your needs and circumstances. Is your original goal realistic?

(g) Strategic Implementation (put the plan into practice):

- Have a training programme
- Start training

(h) Strategic Control (monitor progress, take corrective action):

- Monitor progress against plan
- Have some strategic milestones (e.g. run a half marathon mid-year, etc.)

Exercise 1.5: Suggested (Outline) Solution

In preparing a draft solution, an account of some of the issues which might be considered is given in outline only. You have not been given enough information to prepare a detailed plan!

(a) **Mission might be** to provide adequate healthcare for citizens, or basic healthcare at a reasonable cost. (Where might you find the HSE mission?)

(b) **Objectives** Reduce waiting lists by x% each year/implement new cancer strategy/ achieve cost savings in line with funding availability.

(c) **Environmental analysis:**

- Private competition and prices, e.g. VHI Drug availability and costs
- Rising patient expectations
- Deteriorating public finances – move away from co-location model to more traditional approach?

(d) **Position Audit:**

- Number and quality of staff (and other resources)
- Level of funding committed
- Waiting lists
- Performance measures (Administration costs as % of total expenditure)
- Appropriate structures and culture
- Need to rationalise legacy administrative staff

(e) **Strategic options** might include:

- Remuneration options linked to performance
- Investment in technology, buildings, etc.

(f) **Implementation:**

- Cultural change programmes
- Establishing systems (IT etc)

(g) **Strategic control:**

- Key Performance Indicators
- Balanced Scorecard

Exercise 1.6: Suggested Solution

Google Google operates in a rapidly changing and dynamic environment in terms of its technology and altering business model. An emergent approach to strategy which can quickly adapt to this changing environment is likely to be appropriate. It is unlikely that the Google head office could understand all the trends in the markets in which it operates.

Irish Rail Irish Rail operates in a relatively stable (and declining!) market. It is heavily unionised with significant influence from the State. A rational model might be adopted though, given the range of stakeholders involved, an incremental strategy might be used in practice.

A Research institute It is not clear the type of environment and level of change facing the Institute. Perhaps a rational ('top down') strategy is appropriate.

It should be apparent that it is not possible to be dogmatic – we need to consider the strengths and weaknesses of each organisation and the nature of the environment in which it operates.

CHAPTER 2 – SUGGESTED SOLUTIONS

Exercise 2.1: Personal Goal or Vision for Five Years' Time

Any vision for the future should be balanced. It is not possible to be precise but this vision might cover:

- **Career goals** What else do you see yourself in? How will this develop?
- **Physical dimension goals** What are your financial goals? (not just salary, but pension, healthcare, etc.), health goals, dietary goals, etc.?
- **Social dimension** What social network will you pursue? How will you keep in touch with current friends and family? Social activities and hobbies?
- **Spiritual dimension** What are your key values? How will you seek to develop these in your life? What about giving 'something back'? How might your religious or spiritual values colour what type of person you want to become?
- **Learning dimension** Developing yourself means learning and developing new skills and competencies – CPD requirement, further study to prepare for your next step, etc.

If you wish to develop these ideas further, a good book is Covey's *First Things First*, Franklin Covey (Publishers).

The clearer the picture you have, the more committed you will be to this vision/objective and the greater likelihood that you will achieve it.

Exercise 2.2: Suggested Solution

- Reason for existence/purpose: to be a cosmetic company
- Strategy: Go in the opposite direction to other cosmetic companies. How?
- Values: To be honest (and presumably against animal testing, etc.)
- Policy: To be ethical in all they do

(You will note that there is some overlap between the four elements all of which may not be present in all mission statements.)

Exercise 2.3: Suggested Solution

- To make people happy: Walt Disney
- Beat Coke: Pepsi
- Absolutely, positively overnight: Federal Express
- Undisputed leader in world travel: British Airways

Exercise 2.4: Suggested Solution

No solution is provided to this exercise. If a mission is alive, it needs to be visible, lived out and shared through 'work stories' of our heroes. On joining an organisation, you should be inducted into this mission and we need to recommit to this periodically!

Exercise 2.5: Suggested Solution

No answer is provided. Nonetheless, a clear mission is one that should energise and motivate you. What gives you passion or meaning in your life? If you can tap into this you will be motivated. Do note the different elements identified covering the different elements of your life, your work (career), your social (and family) dimension, your spiritual (legacy) dimension reflected in your voluntary work or church membership. What behaviour is needed to ensure that the words you hope for are realised?

Exercise 2.6: Suggested Solution

For example, you might have identified your role as a student: the objective here is presumably to pass your FAE. Other roles might include such things as: your role as an employee (where would you identify the objectives of this?), son or daughter, member of a club or society, church, etc.

You will quickly note that you have potential conflicts between the different roles and their objectives. How will you manage these conflicts?

Exercise 2.7: Suggested Solution

There is no answer to this exercise. You might recognise the need to appreciate:

- The importance of keeping your objectives in mind
- Ensuring you know what exactly your boss understands by the goals in terms of results, actions and behaviours
- The need to monitor progress
- What extra training or resources are needed to meet the goals.

Exercise 2.8: Suggested Solution – Outline Only

You might consider each of the four categories of employee in terms of their differing preferences towards:

- Desire to help people (altruistic reasons) which is likely to be a key motivator. Professional areas of interest – e.g. consultants who are interested in research or their speciality.
- Status in the hierarchy within the hospital. Doctors and consultants have a very high status. Porters can use their disruptive power to influence their power.

- Future prospects/career: Porters often have long years of service which could impact on loyalty to the institution.
- Money and other rewards may or may not be motivators.
- A social sense of belonging: social workers often have a desire to work for the common good of society.
- Commitment to a public service such as healthcare.

Exercise 2.9: Suggested Solution

The answer here is potentially subjective. Your answer may have made other judgements or assumptions. It is important that you explain your answer!

Low interest and power Presumably people in Dublin may fit this category, unless they have a personal connection or are an environmental activist.

Low interest and high power Government and relevant governmental department and agencies have the power to stop the mining but may have low interest unless local pressure has impacted on them or the law is being broken. Providing them with the appropriate evidence to demonstrate compliance with the law, for example, may be enough.

High interest and low power The local community through which the gas will pass would typically fit this category, as will environmental activists. Shell should ensure that they are informed of the impact on them and how the law is complied with, and the potential benefits of the project in terms of jobs and infrastructure improvement. (What happens to these people's power if they are willing to go to jail and become martyrs?)

High power and interest Presumably, the local authority (Mayo County Council) will need to be satisfied that all regulations, health and safety laws and planning conditions have been complied with and will wish to see evidence of same.

Exercise 2.10: Suggested Solution

1. The mission statement appears to be contradictory. On the one hand, it seeks to maximise shareholder wealth, whilst on the other it seems to also act ethically. Any mine, by its nature, will generate significant environmental impacts and, if the company seeks to maximise shareholder wealth, it is likely to save money in a way that might undermine the environmental objective.
2. Using the criteria above:
   (a) Is it legal? The company has received planning permission and appears to have acted legally. However, the lobbying may not have been ethical (for example were bribes used?).
   (b) Is it truthful? We are not given any information to assess this. Press releases and other media interactions should always be truthful.

(c) Is it fair to all concerned? This is a high standard to uphold. The company cannot meet and respond to the satisfaction of all the conflicting stakeholder preferences. It should be enough to demonstrate that these were considered, and appropriate balanced decisions were made, instead of just focusing on narrow self-interest alone.

(d) Is the behaviour defendable (to your mother for example)? Not too much information is given here. Perhaps the waste water lagoons could contaminate the water supply. Such actions would hardly be defendable.

(e) It is sustainable? Mining is rarely sustainable in the "green" meaning of the word.

You should appreciate the difficult balancing act that is normally needed. This is rarely easy.

CHAPTER 3 – SUGGESTED SOLUTIONS

Exercise 3.1: Suggested Solution

Can you recall:

- The number of hands?
- The form of the date?
- The brand?
- The colour?

Conclusion If this is something you look at every day, what does this say about your ability to read the environment?

Exercise 3.2: Possible Solution

Typical issues might be:

Political and Legal

- Impact of legislation including the smoking ban on outlets and on pub and off licence opening hours.
- Impact of drink driving laws' enforcement and attitudes to drink driving.
- Promotion of moderate consumption of alcohol moving to a state agency. ('Drink Aware' is funded by the industry and, traditionally, the drinks industry has lobbied the Government strongly.)

Economic

- Impact of economic downturn on consumption of beer and alcohol generally.
- Threat of tax increases may moderate demand or alter consumption patterns.
- Cheap imports and cross-border shopping within the EU.
- Switch from on trade to off-licence, especially since the smoking ban.
- Increased competition and concentration of major brands, as well as more specialised local brewing.
- Changing demographics – ageing population, immigration, etc. impacting on changing tastes and consumption patterns.

Social

- Changing tastes and preferences (wine and spirits are becoming more popular).
- Different attitudes to alcohol and healthy lifestyle may impact on demand for beer.

- Changing drinking habits (time and place) and choice (see above).
- Less loyalty to major brands (and opting for specialised imported beers or local microbreweries, for example).

Technology

- Widget can technology
- Impact of microbrewery technology

Environmental

- Possible recycling initiatives to handle cans, bottles and brewery waste
- Possible banning of alcohol advertising

Exercise 3.3: Suggested Solution

Political and Legal

- Changes in legislation and increased regulation will create career opportunities in areas such as compliance, internal control, etc.
- Greater regulation increases the possibility of a lapse in competence leading to action by CARB.
- Ongoing legal changes (National, EU, industry, etc.) result in a continued need to update one's skills and undertake CPD.

Economic

- The current recession has impacted on salaries and prospects in Ireland. Oversees opportunities are possibly brighter in the short-term.
- In Ireland, multinational inward investment/high tech areas remain buoyant.
- International financial services are likely to remain buoyant, though local banking prospects have deteriorated.
- Focus on compliance, IT security, etc. is likely to remain a high demand activity.
- Insolvency/restructuring practices are very busy.

Social

- There is a greater desire for work–life balance.
- Auditors are under greater scrutiny post the financial crisis.
- There is an increased focus on compliance.
- CARB/Regulator/ODCE roles are seen as increasingly important.
- Accountancy is becoming a regulated sector/profession.

Technology

- Increasingly complex IT systems may lead to more IT security roles.
- New technologies create a need for Chartered Accountants to keep up to date and creating opportunities for career, etc.

Exercise 3.4: Suggested Solution

Political and Legal The material provided is silent on possible changes in legislation, taxation or other political factors. Information on the recent laws passed by the Oireachtas is available at www.irishstatutebook.ie. The Website for the European Union might be accessed to see what other laws or directives are planned. Any changes in the law are likely to impact on all opticians equally, so it is unlikely to be significant but may create additional costs or requirements to be followed. However, the company may be breaching the law in the area of its hiring of non-nationals. This is a matter that needs to be regularised soonest, given the reputational and legal exposure the company could face.

Economic The economy appears to have grown rapidly in recent years, though following the recent credit crunch and housing slowdown the rate of growth is falling. Spending by 20 to 30-year-olds is expected to hold up, however. Indications of future economic prospects are likely to impact on consumer spending and, ultimately, our profitability. Inflation is another area we should look at, as this will impact on our cost base. Currency movements, such as the strengthening Euro, should result in lower imported costs which is a positive development. Information on economic prospects are available from the ESRI (www.esri.ie) or other forecasters and most of the major banks. Greater levels of unemployment could result in lower demand.

Social The glasses market has benefited from a shift from glasses being seen as a functional product to a "must-have" designer item. Consumers want convenience in terms of accessing the product and are often "time poor". With a greater shift to heightened consumerism, many customers want unique personalised products rather than traditional ones. This is likely to be a challenge for the company. Trade magazines and the Internet might provide additional insight.

Technology impacts on the products themselves (what they are made of, how they are produced, etc.) and how the service is provided (how quickly and the interface between eye tests and sales). Customers shopping around on the Internet is an example of another trend. Other developments include disposable contact lenses and laser surgery, both of which could reduce demand for glasses. Trade magazines and the Internet might provide additional insight.

Exercise 3.5: Suggested Solution

Barriers to Entry

The deregulation of the airline industry created a reduction in the traditional barriers to entry, with the possible bypassing of restrictive structures. This change was supported by a number of other developments, including:

- **Access to finance** via leasing arrangements (major companies such as Guinness Peat Aviation and GE provided significant finance avoiding the need to borrow directly from banks).

- **Opening up of secondary airports** The reduced security needs within Europe following the end of the "cold war" meant there were a significant number of airfields available as secondary airports that bypassed the controlled air slots as major hubs.

- **Expansion of EU** The increase in EU Member States created demands for expanded routes to smaller venues.

Competitive Rivalry

The competitive rivalry historically was characterised by "cosy cartel" style arrangements with high fares (the Dublin to London route was the highest yielding route in the world at one stage).

The advent of low-cost carriers created fierce competitive rivalry between the new aggressive low cost carriers and the traditional carriers. Air flights went from being exclusive to common practice. The low-cost carriers themselves competed against one another selectively.

Power of Suppliers

The power of traditional suppliers to airlines such as plane manufacturers, airports (who control slots) and fuel providers were greatly weakened by the rapid expansion of a number of successful carriers.

Power of Customers

Initially, the power of customers was low relative to the success of Ryanair. However, customers were given greater choice and an ability to take shorter holidays and weekend breaks. The arrival of the Internet increased customer power somewhat too, though the fragmented nature of individual power has meant a lowering of customer power generally.

Threat of Substitute

The substitutes to air flight such as ferries and trains have struggled to compete with the low cost/high volume model of Ryanair and similar carriers.

Based on your analysis, what are the key changes that have taken place?

The power of the cartel was replaced by significant threats from new entrants and the disruptive effects of expanded demand. The threat of new entrants, coupled with the increased competition, were the dominant forces in the competitive arena.

Exercise 3.6: Suggested Solution

The accountancy profession market can probably be divided into two main segments: 'Big 4' and smaller practices. In answering this, the focus is on the latter segment.

Barriers to Entry

There are limited barriers to entry; at present, anyone can call themselves an accountant, though clearly 'chartered accounting' is a regulated area. There are also significant threats from outsourcing of work overseas and greater competition from accounting technicians at the small client end of the market for accounting services.

Competitive Rivalry

There is a high level of rivalry given the low barriers to entry and the limited scope to differentiate.

Power of Suppliers

The office rental market (as an input to the business) is relatively favourable, given surplus capacity. The cost of labour is also favourable in the current recession.

Power of Customers

Customers' ability to afford (and pay) for services has caused pressure on fees. It is easy for customers to switch service to another accountant.

Threat of Substitutes

The advent of sophisticated accounts packages which are easy to use, plus the increased availability of services offered by accounting technicians, all act to depress rates.

Exercise 3.7: Suggested Solution

Factor Conditions

Ireland's position in competitive terms has been strengthened through developments in the advanced factor conditions:

- Significant investment in education ('free' secondary education from the late 1960s onwards, investment in universities in the 1970s onwards, abolition of third-level fees in the 1990s and, more recently, an expansion in State funding for the 4th level sector (research)).

- Investment in infrastructure addressing the historical deficits.
- State support and tax breaks for research and development.

Demand Conditions

The Irish market alone is small and unlikely to offer the opportunity for economies of scale. However, through access to EU markets and the use of the Internet, such opportunities are possible.

Related and Support Industries

The financial services sector in Ireland has benefited from the support of a strong legal, accounting and tax infrastructure, as well as regulation (now questioned). The ability to amend State legislation to develop niche markets has been a sou0rce of competitive advantage. The big pharmaceutical and chemical sectors were targeted by the IDA and successfully attracted to Ireland.

Firm Strategy Structure and Rivalry

IDA Ireland has sought to attract successful international companies to locate their European HQ in Ireland. Rivalry amongst players in Ireland has resulted in the expansion of the financial services sector outside of Dublin to the regions.

Exercise 3.8: Suggested Solution

See solution to **BWF Case – Exercise**, Appendix 2 – Black & White Foods – Suggested Solutions, at the end of this Toolkit.

Exercise 3.9: Suggested Solution

As each solution will be individual/depend on the clients selected, no answer is provided here.

CHAPTER 4 – SUGGESTED SOLUTIONS

Exercise 4.1: Suggested Solution

As this is a personal exercise, no formal solution is provided. Ideally, you would start this exercise with a list of the requirements for a specific job. In the context of your work, your strengths and weaknesses might cover:

Core Competencies

- Technical knowledge of particular areas (accounting standards, or tax).
- Evidenced skills in, say, undertaking research, problem solving, etc.
- General business common sense and benefits derived from this in terms of adding value to clients, etc.

Personal Skills/Characteristics

- Ability to work in teams/manage teams
- Ability to motivate, monitor and appraise
- Numeracy, analytical skills, IT skills, etc.
- Ethical behaviour/practice – how might this be evidenced?

Experience

- Client experience
- Sectorial experience
- Ireland/overseas

Other

- Other areas that you can draw on to supplement key skills (hobbies, education, travel, languages, etc.)

Exercise 4.2: Suggested Solution

In general, the key success factors in any organisation are generally instantly recognisable.

Coca-Cola's strengths are in the area of marketing, in particular brand development and promotion at national and global levels. (What characteristics do you associate with the product based on the advertising messages you have heard?) The brand is a truly global one.

Coca-Cola's distribution is carried out by distributors who purchase the concentrate from Coca-Cola directly. As consumers, we expect the Coca-Cola product to be satisfactory in terms of quality, but this is hardly a defining characteristic.

Exercise 4.3: Suggested Solution

No solution is provided for this exercise. You might score the organisation against its nearest competitors. Such an analysis is likely to be subjective, but can yield key insights in terms of how we compare with our competitors.

Exercise 4.4: Suggested Solution

Materials

Probably not a key area, given Ryanair operates in a service industry.

Men

On the positive side, we might identify:

- Reliance on contract staff
- Non-unionised
- Low-cost wages

(Consider impact of above on morale and labour turnover.)

Management

- Dominant chief executive: Is he too dominant?
- What about the range of management skills and experience required to run an airline (you may not be sure of the answers and may need to do some research)?

Machinery

- Ryanair has standardised its fleet using Boeing 737s.

Money

- Ryanair finances remain strong: with a low cost base, they have consistently outperformed other leading European airlines.
- Ancillary income has grown significantly, e.g. car hire, etc.

Makeup

- Consider Ryanair's relative culture, structure, brand:
    - o The message of "low cost airline" is constantly reinforced; and
    - o The culture of low cost and low customer service is seen as reinforcing the low cost base.

Methods

- Efficient turnaround of plane
- Heavy usage of planes
- Non-unionised staff
- Outsourcing as needed

Markets

- Ryanair is popular with individuals taking short breaks rather than traditional business travellers.

MIS

- Ryanair presumably measures its performance against key measures:

  o Yield
  o Occupancy
  o Cost per flight

(Where you have gaps: how might you seek to close this gap? Who might be able to assist you?)

Exercise 4.5: Suggested Solution

Sources of information could include:

- Publicly available information:

  o Annual reports
  o Public plans or strategy documents
  o Website
  o Trade organisations
  o Websites/brochures/reports
  o Regulator reports for sector where available

- Secondary information:

  o Media searches
  o Google or equivalent

- Other:

  o Friends or acquaintances who have worked there
  o People who work in the industry
  o International trends in the sector: likely impact on local market?

Exercise 4.6: Suggested Solution

- Black and white televisions: Decline stage
- Digital TV: Growth stage
- Flat screen TV: Growth stage
- Web broadcasting: Introduction stage
- 3D Television: Introduction stage
- Interactive TV: Covered above

Any classification by nature is subjective. You may wish to challenge some of the above. Any assessment will change as time goes on.

Exercise 4.7: Suggested Solution

You should identify:

- Products have a limited life, so we need to plan for replacements
- As products age, different actions are needed to market these and we need to adapt our marketing efforts accordingly in terms of product, price, promotion and place
- We need to have a balanced portfolio of products

Exercise 4.8: Suggested Outline Solution

Possible options might include:

- Spin off products
- New improved design and/or packaging
- Reduced price
- Market extension
- Heavy promotion

Exercise 4.9: Suggested Solution

The key challenge is having sufficient resources to support the development of stars and question marks. Possible solutions might include disposing of surplus resources or raising funding (perhaps by selling one of the stars) to generate sufficient funds. Alternatively, options such as franchising might be appropriate. At the end of the day, a cash cow is needed to provide long-term funding.

Here we need to recognise that ultimately all cash cows will decline and there is a need to develop some new products to replace them. This might be done through product development, acquisition of new products or a joint venture.

Exercise 4.10: Suggested Solution

Comparing Ryanair and Aer Lingus (Outline only): you might have compared the experience against the following:

Check In

- Number of staff: At check in and to board plane?
- Automated check-in?
- Use of Internet check-in?

Handle your Baggage

- Handling charges?
- Restrictions on baggage?
- Flexible staff arrangements?
- Outsourcing of baggage handling?

Boarding the Plane

- Preferential seating?
- Charging for same?
- Systems to support capture of passenger details?

On Flight Experience, etc.

- No seat pocket
- Advertising on board
- Sales on board
- Space on board

Exercise 4.11: Suggested Solution

Given the limited nature of the information, any assessment is going to be subjective and open to debate.

Element of the value chain	Assessment of Specky for Eyes	Assessment of competitors
Primary Activities		
Inbound logistics	Limited information given, though it appears that receipt of supplies and parts is slower than competitors	Competitors appear to be able to get supplies in fast and thereby cut delivery times. They may also hold a greater range of stocks

(continued)

Operations	Glasses selection and assembly is traditional and slow	Have adopted newer technologies and methods to speed up the sales and delivery process
Outbound logistics	Not a significant factor in this case	n/a
Marketing and sales	Traditionally very little marketing – a weakness. Some additional marketing planned	Competitors have built a high degree of brand recognition
After sales service	High degree of loyalty may be indicative of service, though information is limited	Appear to focus on good products and fast turnaround time. Whilst it is hard to be specific, perhaps they are stronger here: more information (market research) would help
Support activities		
Procurement	Company has sourced its products from a varied range of suppliers	Presumably similar
Technology development	Slow adoption of new technologies and processes	Technologies used as a differentiator and have highlighted conservatism of Specky for Eyes
Human resource management	Paternalistic style of management, limited evidence of staff development or performance measurement. Remuneration is traditional and unlikely to motivate. High level of loyalty	Limited information given but assume younger, more 'energetic' staff – with more progressive policies in terms of progression, performance measurement and remuneration
Management planning/ firm infrastructure	High level of central control – probably too much control which can be demotivating	Little information given

In conclusion, Specky for Eyes comes out relatively unfavourably in our comparison. In practice, you would like to see market research, talk to customers, etc., to confirm your views. The existing strategic position of Specky for Eyes does not appear to be viable in the longer term.

CHAPTER 5 – SUGGESTED SOLUTIONS

Exercise 5.1: Suggested Solution to Specky for Eyes SWOT analysis

STRENGTHS	WEAKNESSES
New energetic and experienced COO	Limited marketing expertise in a market that is increasingly image conscious
Range of stores on high street locations	Declining profitability and margins
Range of traditional products	Market may perceive product range to be dated and unattractive
Healthy cash position, no borrowings	Slow adoption of new technologies and delivery systems
Established range of suppliers	Traditional pay structures based on scales, little performance measurement or rewards
Loyal staff, with long service	Well established routines, perhaps staff are not open to change
Good reputation for service and reliability, though this may have diminished somewhat in recent times	Little thought given to the planned exit from the business by John Specky

THREATS	OPPORTUNITIES
Economic slowdown with reduced consumer spending	20 to 30-year-old segment appears to offer opportunities
Increasing competition from a range of strong competitors	Possible adoption of newer technologies
Consumer preference for accessible stores and increasing traffic means that time is short	Development of newer designer range of glasses
Possible legal exposure due to hiring procedures with non-nationals	Endorsement of product by music artist
	Enhanced service through inclusion of opticians on site

Summary of the Three Key Strategic Challenges Facing Specky for Eyes

The chain is at a point of significant change which may result in new opportunities or perhaps decline if not handled correctly. A number of the key challenges may be summarised as follows:

- The planned retirement of John Specky and his exit from the business is likely to be affected by his long tenure, and staff may find the change traumatic. This may result in a greater level of introspection in an organisation that appears to have an introverted culture when a more external market culture is needed.

- The company needs to rapidly decide how it will handle new market challenges through greater market awareness and also new product ranges and work practices. This requires new training and skill sets to be developed urgently.

- Staff management needs to be examined. The culture appears to be quite paternalistic and linked to remuneration and the performance measurement system will need to be reviewed so that staff can be better motivated. New hires may help.

Exercise 5.2: Suggested Solution

Build on Our Strengths to Tackle Opportunities

After 9/11, Ryanair used its strong financial resources to purchase airplanes at a significant discount. Boeing had seen a significant decline in orders which Ryanair was able to use to its advantage. When the market later picked up, Ryanair disposed of surplus planes at a profit.

Convert Weaknesses into Strengths

Arguably, Ryanair's poor customer service can be considered to be a weakness. Yet, they celebrate the impact of this on their ability to maintain low prices. Poor customer service is presented as a "badge of honour".

Convert Threats into Opportunities

After 9/11, the global flying market was in turmoil with flights grounded. Ryanair launched a major marketing drive with cheap flights to get people flying again. Most traditional carriers were slow to respond to the threat. This rapid response reflects their flexibility.

Tackle Weaknesses to see off Threats

The power of the EU to restrict Ryanair's modus operandi, for example requiring improved refunds when cancellations occur, compelling grants to be repaid or blocking the Aer Lingus bid, reflect Ryanair's inability to lobby at EU level. Strengthening their lobbying position could be seen as tackling the weakness to see off the threat.

CHAPTER 6 – SUGGESTED SOLUTIONS

Exercise 6.1: Suggested Solution

The case material does not indicate that Specky for Eyes has structured its business in such a way as to keep costs at a minimum. Indeed, they appear to have relied on their product offering as a means of differentiating themselves in the market. Unfortunately, the areas on which they have differentiated no longer seem to be valued by the customer. The only question is whether they are following a broad base or focused approach to differentiation. As they are focused on the Dublin market only, it appears that the approach is focused differentiation.

Exercise 6.2: Suggested Solution

Possible ways in which airlines might differentiate include:
- Flight routes (short haul or long haul)
- Principal airports or secondary airports served
- Range of service offerings (economy class, business class, etc.)
- Degree of in-flight service
- Size of seat and space around the seat
- Timing of flights
- Scheduled vs chartered
- Customer care (before and after)
- Booking system
- Price

Contrast these actions in terms of what a cost leadership or differentiation strategy might do.

	Cost leader (low-cost carrier)	Differentiator
Flight routes (short haul or long haul)		
Principal airports or secondary airports served		
Range of class of seat offered		
Degree of in-flight service		
Size of seat and space around the seat		
Timing of flights		
Scheduled vs chartered		
Customer care (before and after)		
Booking system		
Price		

Exercise 6.3: Suggested Solution

Penetration

Perhaps through increased market spending on advertising Specky could seek to increase its market share.

Product Development

This might involve the introduction of a new range of products such as contact lenses, or perhaps new designer frames made from unusual materials.

Market Development

This would perhaps involve Specky opening a new branch outside of Dublin, or selling through new dispensaries located in leading department stores within shopping centres.

Diversification

This would involve Specky moving out of the business altogether, perhaps by selling the properties.

Exercise 6.4: Suggested Solution

Applying the Ansoff matrix to your career as a Chartered Accountant:

Penetration

This would typically involve you remaining in the same area of work and in the same industry, building up additional depth of industry/relevant technical knowledge and experience.

Service/Product Development

This would cover you developing a new product or service targeted at your current client or internal customers. Being seen to be innovative and developing reports or tools to assist the users of information will help you to advance your career.

Market Development

Here, you take your existing knowledge/skills/competencies, etc., and apply them in a new or related market segment. Perhaps you have been involved in an IT project and have learnt skills which can be applied in a new market.

Diversification

From a career perspective, this would involve a move sideways away from 'core accountancy/tax/audit' to a support role in an unrelated industry perhaps.

Exercise 6.5: Suggested Solution

Specky for Eyes could expand organically by using its own resources and (perhaps borrowings) to increase the range of stores over a wider locality. Alternatively, it could purchase or takeover another chain in, say, Galway. Otherwise, this expansion might be achieved through a joint venture or a franchise arrangement with existing companies in Galway.

CHAPTER 8 – SUGGESTED SOLUTIONS

Exercise 8.1: Suggested Solution

A key issue in any submission should be that the writer has considered the lender's perspective rather than an insider/management perspective. Such a document needs to be balanced and, hopefully, cover all aspects required but not in too much detail. Focusing on the key lender concerns and addressing them should ensure that the loan request/business plan achieves its purpose. Some of the concerns of the lender are:

- **Track record** The lender will wish to see that the product has an established customer profile and market. Does the product have superior features or performance to support this?

- **Credible projections** The projections should be realistic and bear some relationship to the previous performance. A 'hockey stick' projection with success in, say, year three or four will cause worries from a lender perspective. One way of providing some comfort might be to present a range of alternatives. Alternatively, some sensitivity analysis and breakeven measures may be sufficient. A focus on free cash flow rather than just profit is likely.

- **Management capacity** The lender will wish to have the comfort of knowing that the management have the experience and track record to ensure success. Indications on how management will monitor and control progress will be an additional expectation.

- **Market rather than technical focus** A lender will want to understand how the product will succeed in the market. Is there a clear need or niche which the product is addressing? Often technical/entrepreneurial individuals can focus on technical matters which may not be critical in the market.

- **Lender's needs** A lender will wish to be assured that appropriate security is available, as well as potential exit routes in due course. For example, venture capital investors may seek Board representation. The lender will also look at the capital required, how it is structured and the timing issues required.

Exercise 8.2: Suggested Solution

(This is a fuller answer than is required – it is included for reference purposes)

1. *Company details*

   Typical questions you will need to be able to answer are:
   - **The nature of the business** How did the business come about and its development in summary form.
   - **Progress to date** A summary of the key achievements to date. Whilst past performance is clearly no guarantee of future performance, the financier is likely to be reassured by a steady and progressive record rather than a history of one crisis after another.

- **Company name and location** Typical issues to be considered include:

  o What is your company called and other associated trading names, domain names and key brands?

  o Where is your main location of business? Or details of multiple sites if appropriate.

  o What is the nature of the business?

  o In summary, what is your current trading position?

- **Ownership & legal status** Consider:

  o Who are the key personnel/owners?

  o What is the legal form of the business?

  o Are there any legal issues affecting the company (licensing arrangements or major (current) law suits for example)?

2. *Market potential*

Key issues cover:

- **Geographical area** What geographical area does your company serve or plan to serve? Are there any measures as to market size and growth potential? What are the influences of market growth?

- **Customer characteristics** What are the key characteristics of the customers? What factors influence customer purchasing decisions? How does your product meet these expectations in, say, terms of market share or standing?

- **Competitive advantage** What is the basis of the company's competitive advantage; how do the company's existing products exploit the current market? How will this be sustained?

3. *Products or services details*

Key issues are:

- What are your main products or services?

- What do these products do? (Remember a technical product may not be understood.)

- How might the products change in the future?

Commentary

The level of detail needed here will depend on the product (or service) to be funded and its state of development. It will also depend on the audience needs and, in general, too much technical detail should be avoided. A key issue will be the state of play – is the product ready for marketing? Or is there significant work to be done prior to launch? If the product is still at prototype stage, then it is important that the reader appreciates the next steps to be taken and how long this may take.

If a product has unique aspects or features, then there is likely to be merit in protecting this through copyright and patents. Details of such protection should be provided. Details of the production processes by which the unique features are created may be outlined.

Most organisations will have a portfolio of products at various stages in their life cycle and a profile of each major product grouping can be included.

4.   *The Competition*

Some key questions to answer might be:

- Who are our competitors or potential competitors?
- What are their strengths and weaknesses?
- How is our market currently divided?
- What market share do we have? How is this changing?
- How do we maintain and sustain our competitive advantage? Do we have any market research to support our claims?
- What barriers to entry might exist?

5.   *Marketing and Sales Strategy*

This relates to how we plan to market and sell our products. Some key questions to be answered might include:

- How do you want your customers to think of your company in the market? (Think of Avis "we try harder", for example.)
- How will you market your products? Advertising? Mail order? Direct selling? Sales-staff? Online rather than Internet?
- What expected costs and spend are planned?
- What other activities or promotional activities are planned? What will this cost?
- How are our sales teams organised and rewarded?

Commentary

The business plan should include extracts of market research that has been undertaken and supports the existence of the expected market. It may not always be possible to do this and some new inventions may take time to create and build a potential demand.

Any marketing plan should cover the "4 Ps" of product, price, promotion and place. These separate elements will need to be adapted as a product (hopefully) succeeds and moves through the product life cycle.

6. *Operations*

You will need to consider and demonstrate the operations of the company and how it functions – hopefully assuring the reader that you know how to run the business successfully. Any change in strategy is likely to require some changes in the operations.

Operations typically include:

- Location and facilities: Premises are a key asset and may need to be developed to meet our future needs. As these may be used as security for a loan, you should consider any available valuations, access to transport and other legal issues (if any)
- Purchasing processes and supplier management
- Production/manufacturing (including outsourcing arrangements)
- Equipment and technology
- Stock management/order fulfilment/customer service
- Quality control and assurance processes

Your document should outline all of the above in broad simple terms.

- Are there any particular areas where we have superiority? How do we compare to our competitors?
- Are there any "state of the art" facilities or processes?
- What are our key challenges and how will we address them?
- Are there bottlenecks or issues which we are seeking to address?

7. *Management Team*

Some details on the key managers, how they became involved and their backgrounds and expertise is likely to be needed. Typical issues which will need to be addressed are:

- Who are the key managers in the team?
- Can you provide a summary CV for each of the key staff?
- What about your future management needs?
- How is the management team organised?
- Who are the Board members? Provide details of any non-execs
- Who are the key business advisors?

The section of the plan detailing the ownership and management will expand on the details above. Summarised CVs are likely to be included here or as an appendix.

These should focus on relevant achievements rather than a chronological list of jobs. If there are weaknesses in the current team, these should be highlighted with proposed solutions. Often organisations have weaknesses at an early stage of development, and we would wish to see this addressed. The overall team needs to be sufficiently balanced.

In preparing a document for such a submission, you should consider what key characteristics you would expect to be present in the various members of the management team. Whilst it is difficult to capture all the characteristics in the CV, lenders will expect a record of achievement and resilience.

8. *Future Strategy*

- What are the key developments planned over the next, say, five years?
- What key milestones are to be achieved in terms of key measures such as turnover, profit, staffing, etc.? When?
- What are the key risks which impinge on our strategy, and how will we mitigate these?
- What exit plan do we envisage for any backer, e.g. trade sale, MBO, flotation etc.?

9. *Financials*

- **Aims and financial forecasts** What are the financial and market targets? Summarised financial forecasts for sales, profits and cash flows will be needed.
- **Funding requirements** How much funding is needed and in what form? Are there any timing issues?
- **Expected returns** What level of return can the lender expect to achieve? There should be a clear relationship between past performance and planned performance. Lenders will compare the earnings, margins and cash flow historically to what is expected. A "hockey stick pattern" is likely to give rise to many questions!
- **Detailed financial projections** As you would expect, these should include (probably in appendices):
  - o Income statement (projections)
  - o Projected balance sheets
  - o Projected cash flow statements

It may be appropriate to have a range of projections to allow for different possible scenarios. At a minimum, sensitivity analysis is needed, supported by such computations as breakeven points.

Sufficient allowance needs to be made for the initial investment (including contingencies) as well as working capital. It may be helpful to include appropriate ratios, particularly where loan covenants may be required.

In terms of the financial requirements, most lenders will wish to understand and see the existing investors committing to the project financially. This gives them the appropriate confidence in the investors' commitment to the business.

Exercise 8.3: Suggested Solution

Understand the objective:

- Discuss the objective with your manager and learn his/her preferences for how the strategy might be developed.
- Review the full strategy to gain an understanding of the big picture and any other trends or issues.
- Ensure you have top management support.
- Ensure that all goals are aligned to higher goals (management by objectives).

Staff appraisals:

- Agree staff goals which are aligned to the departmental goals.
- Highlight any training needs that have to be met in order for the goals to be achieved.
- Clarify any resources that are needed to enable the goals to be met.
- Once staff have the the necessary training and resources, they should be able to meet the goals.
- Agree review dates to monitor progress.
- Agree any rewards which may arise.

Discuss the objective with your team:

- Organise a planning session with the team to develop a sales plan to achieve your objective.
- Compare the planned performance against the historic trends. Are there any likely problems?

Resource plans:

- Identify critical factors for success.
- Identify how resources will be deployed.

Consider interaction with other departments:

- What are the financial requirements that need to be met? Liaison with the finance department may be needed.
- How can increased sales be accommodated by our production department?
- Are there any staff constraints that need to be managed? Liaison with the HR department may be needed.

Processes:

- What are the detailed actions to be taken to increase sales?
- Who is responsible and accountable?
- What changes in processes are needed?

- How are the changes to be communicated?
- What training may be needed in the process changes?

In this case, we have not been given details of what is required, so we have been relatively high level in the outline above.

Exercise 8.4: Suggested Solution

Possible answer (outline only):

Failure	Possible action
Limited staff involvement in the development: no buy in from the sales team evident	Assuming we wish to proceed with the project, we should re-establish a project team with involvement from all key players
No evidence of top management sponsorship or champion	Top management to restate importance of project and to link this to goals and rewards
Implementation was rushed with loss of user features	User features to be redeveloped (perhaps using prototyping tools)
Training was inadequate	A programme of training to be rolled out considering timing and needs
Errors in the system resulted in a loss of trust	Efforts are needed to rebuild trust in the system
Old system allowed to continue	A defined end date should be established
Reward systems not addressed	Rewards to be aligned with new structures
Communications appear poor	Communications plan to be put in place
Project management appears weak	Train staff in PM techniques
No change management process	Change management process to be part of the project management

CHAPTER 9 – SUGGESTED SOLUTIONS

Exercise 9.1: Suggested Solution

Issues which might be clarified with your client:

1. We do not know the priorities for the AHE or its strategic goals as criteria to be used. This suggests that this matter should be clarified soonest.

2. You should query how the various ratios should be interpreted. For example, for a university to achieve a high percentage of graduates with a first-class honours degree is generally seen as positive, unless standards are not equivalent across universities. High graduate unemployment would generally be seen as unfavourable but is affected by local market conditions.

3. Weightings: No guidance has been given as to whether any criteria/data provided should be given extra weighting.

4. You might consider preferences in terms of how the data might be presented.

Below is a table of comparative performance of the four universities:

University	Belfast	Dublin	Southern	Western
Surplus/Deficit (Note l)				
2011	1	2	3	4
2010	2	3	1	4
Change	1	3	4	2
Grant income (Note 2)	1	1	3	4
Fee income (Note 3)	3	1	2	4
Non-fee income (Note 4)	2	1	3	4
Average student fees (Note 5)	2	3	4	1
Non-national students (Note 6)	4	2	3	1
Lecturing staff/student ratio (Note 7)	3	4	2	1
Support staff to students (Note 8)	4	3	2	1
Attractiveness (Note 9)	4	2	3	1
% achieving 1st (Note 10)	2	3	4	1
% achieving honours degree (Note 11)	2	4	2	1
% drop out (Note 12)	3	4	2	1
Unemployment (Note 13)	3	1	4	1
Lecturer contact hours (Note 14)	4	3	2	1

(*continued*)

Research articles (Note 15)	1	3	4	2
Lecturer salaries (Note 16)	1	3	4	3
Support staff salaries (Note 16)	1	4	3	2
Total score	44	50	56	39
Number of '1's	6	4	1	10

Notes

1. It is difficult to evaluate the performance in terms of surplus and deficit. In simple terms, the four universities have been ranked in order of performance (1 being best/4 being worst) for the two years. A third row entitled "change" ranks the universities in the order of greatest improvement to worst deterioration.

2. For grant income it is assumed that higher grant income is better than less reflecting a greater commercial ethos.

3. Universities have been ranked in terms of size: the assumption being the larger the better. This could be challenged!

4. It is assumed that the more non-fee income the better as this reflects a greater commercial drive in the colleges.

5. Average student fees have been computed as being the total student fees divided by the number of undergraduate and postgraduate students. A higher fee is assumed to be better than a lower one. The figures are (45m/8,750 or €5.14k; 66m/14,907 or €4.43k; 51 m/11,650 or €4.38k; 40m/6,150 or €6.5k). The variation may reflect the higher level of non-national students perhaps.

6. It is assumed that the non-national student intake is seen as adding to the educational "vibrancy" of the college: thus the higher the better!

7. The level of lecturers to students has been computed below. It is assumed that the higher the ratio, the more efficient the university is. This assumption is open to challenge and would be affected by the type of degrees on offer, the level of post graduate studies undertaken, etc.

8. Support staff to student ratio (see table below): it is assumed that the lower the level of support staff the better.

9. Attractiveness is based on the surplus of points on admission over the criteria set. A range of alternatives might be possible here. The Western university achieves a 60 point excess over its own entry criteria, whereas Belfast is at the other extreme. (An alternative might have been to simply take the average points achieved.)

10. It is assumed that all university graduates have equal ability and are marked to the same standard. No inflation of grades is assumed for both first and second class degrees.

11. The first and second class degrees have been combined here.

12. A lower dropout is assumed to be better than a higher dropout rate.

13. A lower unemployment rate is assumed to be better. This is affected by local economic factors and may not necessarily reflect on the universities' performance.

14. A higher number of contact hours is assumed to be better in terms of efficiency. A higher load will impact on the time available to undertake other work, including research, for example, which may not be a good outcome.

15. A higher level of research output is assumed to be better. No indicators have been given as to the quality or ranking of the research. It might be appropriate to adjust the research by the number of lecturers. (Further analysis is probably needed.)

16. A lower salary is deemed to be better from the funding authority viewpoint for both lecturers and support staff.

Workings

University	Belfast	Dublin	Southern	Western
Total students	8,750	14,907	11,650	6,150
Total lecturers	202	410	220	102
Student/lecturers	43.3	36.4	53.0	60.3
Rank	3	4	2	1
Support staff	420	690	450	78
Students/support staff	20.8	21.6	25.9	78.9
Rank	4	3	2	1

Conclusion

On the basis of the lowest score (highest number of '1's), the western university is announced to be the best. The outcome is affected by the assumptions made. Should weightings be applied, the result could change further.

Additional Information

Examples of additional information might include

Full sets of financial information over recent years.

- Copies of plans for development as well as financial plans.
- External assessment reports undertaken.
- Comparisons of possible benchmarks from other countries (e.g. lecturer/student ratios and costs).
- Data is provided on an aggregate basis for the university but should be broken down by faculty, as certain faculties will incur higher costs (e.g. science or medicine will typically cost more than arts faculties).
- Feedback from employers on the graduates' and post graduates' capabilities.

Developing and Rolling Out the Balanced Scorecard

Typical steps in such a project would include:
- Obtain from senior management a copy of the approved terms of reference.
- Consider makeup of team: need for a balance of backgrounds and experience.
- Kick-off meeting of team.
- Outline project plan.
- Gather data – via workshops, focus groups, interviews.
- Analyse data.
- Develop prototype.
- Test prototype with users and redesign as needed.
- Present to management.
- Rollout and train users.
- Operate and monitor.

Change Management

Typical change management issues would include:
- Obtaining top management buy in and support for the project.
- Regular reporting to senior management.
- Communications strategy for all those affected by the development.
- Appropriate training as needed.
- Use of consultants or other change agents.
- Consider cost benefit issues, etc.

APPENDIX 2 – BLACK & WHITE FOODS – SUGGESTED SOLUTIONS

BWF Case – Exercise 1: Suggested Solution

Insights into the External Environment facing Black & White Foods

Prepared by Financial Analyst, ACA

I believe that the external environment facing us in BWF is broadly positive, although not without some risks. I have laid out this briefing paper in terms of both Positive and Negative influences on BWF from the external environment. I would be happy to discuss these in further detail if you wish.

Positive Influences on BWF in the External Environment:

- Spending on food continues to grow despite the recession, meaning we and our customers are better placed than many companies in these recessionary times.
- The food industry is well regarded by the market, making fundraising or additional borrowing easier.
- Changes in demand and growth in new fusion products favours colourant companies such as BWF as new products will require new colours.
- There is increasing demand for organic colourants that we produce.
- The increasing trend towards urbanisation in the world and the growth of 'mega cities' means more Home Meal Replacement (HMR) food, again to the benefit of ingredients companies such as ourselves as more people eat more processed food.
- Increasing taste for Western-style food in India and China will boost demand for our products.
- Ireland has a positive reputation for food production and that will help us in the market.
- There are acquisition opportunities available and as we have little debt we are better placed than many companies to avail of them.
- We are not exposed to the banks to any significant extent and that is a big positive as the banks will penalise those borrowers who breach their borrowing conditions.
- Significant growth is clearly attainable in the market based on our recent track record.
- There is no real pricing pressure from our customers – it helps that we represent such a small part of the overall spend.
- R&D is becoming increasingly important to our customers and that is where BWF is strong.
- We have identified investment opportunities which we could avail of.
- There are opportunities to gain customers with our technologically superior existing products.

- The trend toward outsourcing in the market (as in so many other industries) will provide opportunities for suppliers such as BWF.

- The increasing use of the 'partnership' business model will suit BWF as we are already used to working closely with our customers.

- As suppliers add more value to food company customers the suppliers will become increasingly important trading partners and price will become less of a dominant decision variable, which is good for BWF as we are very unlikely to be the lowest cost producer.

- As food producers acquire ingredients companies opportunities may arise for us to gain customers where some other producers will not buy from a supplier owned by a competitor, particularly in a 'partnership' type arrangement where the supplier is privy to new product ideas or plans.

Notwithstanding the many positive factors in the external environment for BWF, there are also quite a number of negatives in the external environment, as follows:

- Because of food quality scares there is a danger that people will move away from processed foods, despite the convenience.

- There is pressure on consumer spending due to the recession, even on food.

- Ireland is still a high cost manufacturing environment, despite recent progress, and there is a risk that BWF could become increasingly uncompetitive on cost as a result.

- Growing brand power will improve the negotiating position of the food manufacturer and the food retailer at the expense of suppliers.

- Consolidation within the food industry will mean that BWF will become a relatively smaller player with less power in the industry.

- The worldwide trend in manufacturing towards local suppliers and Just In Time systems will work against BWF, where all production is located in Ireland.

- The trend towards acquisitions means that some of our competitors may become part of even larger food groups, locking us out of certain customers.

- The reduced 'time to market' because of the need to develop new products ever faster increases the risk of potential mistakes.

- Increased litigation, particularly in relation to food, means that any development errors could prove very costly.

- The growth in pure ethnic foods will not, in general, suit BWF.

BWF Case – Exercise 2: Suggested Solution

Insights into the key competencies and strategic strengths of Black & White Foods

Prepared by Financial Analyst, ACA

I have set out in the table below the key competencies and strengths of BWF, the future threats to them, and the opportunities to exploit them:

Key competencies and strengths of BWF	Future threats to these key competencies and strengths	Opportunities to exploit these key competencies and strengths
Strong financial position with existing venture capital support	Venture capital could lose interest and become a dissatisfied investor. Venture capital investor could seek to sell their stake to an unsuitable purchaser. Rash decisions (see separate note on strategic options) could erode financial position. Competitors that are part of larger food groups could seek to use their financial strength to reduce prices and force us to lose contracts.	If there is a downturn in the industry our financial strength will help us to survive longer than others, the 'last man standing' principle. We are ideally placed to make acquisitions in a cyclical downturn, when valuations are reduced. We could seek to buy out the VC investors. We can continue to invest in R&D which is becoming more important.
Our R&D capability, particularly as this becomes more important in the industry	Food manufacturers with their own colourant companies may not want to divulge confidential product development ideas to us. There is a greater financial risk with R&D than other types of investment. Conceivably we could lack funds for very heavy R&D although this seems unlikely. The VC investors could object to R&D spending. Because we are so focused in Ireland our R&D could be too local and lose touch with what is happening in the global market. Key staff could be lured away to other competitors.	Continue to invest in R&D. Incentivise and try to tie in key staff, perhaps with long-term incentives such as stock options. Set up a research facility overseas to ensure we are picking up international food trends. Use electronic market research such as 'blogs' to pick up on international trends.

Experience and competence in partnership-type arrangements with customers, particularly as they become more important in the industry.	One publicised breach of customer confidentiality could seriously damage the reputation of BWF. If a new product fails then BWF and the colourants could be regarded as partly to blame, even though this may not be the case. Customers may be reluctant to enter into partnership-type arrangements with companies with which they do not have a formal link, although this has not been a problem in the past.	The fact that BWF are independent of other ingredients companies may work to our advantage as customers without a link to colourant companies may not want to enter partnership-type arrangements sharing confidential information with companies that are linked to competitors. Need an explicit policy for protecting against potential conflicts of interest with different customers. Actively seek out partnership-type arrangements with customers, offering to share staff and bear part of the cost. Stress our experience and success to date in this area in sales or proposal-type arrangements. Actively publicise some successes in this area. Make sure staff see that participation in such a programme improves their chances of advancement.
Quality of our products.	The industry dynamics may change, and cost may become a more important variable than quality – this is relatively unlikely though as the cost of colourants is a tiny part of the overall product cost. Our quality standards could slip, and we have seen in the food industry that one mistake can attract huge attention and do huge reputational damage.	Continue to invest in Quality Control procedures, accepting nothing less than best in class. Look at other industries with high standards, such as aircraft manufacture, and see what can be learned. Put a contingency plan in place to respond if problems do occur.

Consensus decision-making has worked well in the past and prevented any significant errors.	The first risk is that BWF will be too cautious and will miss opportunities. The second risk is that all 20 members of the KMG are involved in the strategy of the company and therefore if any of them were to move to a competitor they could take a lot of potentially valuable information with them.	This approach has served BWF well and I would not recommend that it be changed. I think the KMG need to be aware of the need to move quickly where necessary, and to move quicker than would have been necessary in the past. We have addressed above the need to incentivise and retain key management.

BWF Case – Exercise 3: Suggested Solution

Strategic options for Black & White Foods

Prepared by Financial Analyst, ACA

I have considered the four strategic options outlined by the Marketing Manager and ranked them in terms of their relative attractiveness, as follows:

Strategic option	Ranking of responsiveness to external environment	Ranking in terms of ability to build on key competencies	Overall ranking (highest is best)
Develop cross-shareholding links with a larger food ingredients group	2	3	5
Become a food supplies group	1	2	3
Build a property portfolio	3	1	4
Stay focused on edible colourants	4	4	8

I believe the KMG should consider the following strategic options:

- **Remain in the food colourants industry but internationalise the business** – by looking at setting up both R&D and production facilities overseas.

- **Acquire other specialist food ingredients companies** – perhaps overseas, such as companies producing spices, extra virgin olive oil, etc.
- **Aggressively expand the research function** – perhaps in conjunction with local universities.

The following is a list of action plans and timeframes which the KMG should follow in order to choose the strategic options they should adopt:

Strategic option	Action Plan	Timeframe required
Maintain the existing business model	Review the opportunities linked to the key competencies identified earlier and decide if it is feasible to implement them	Report back to KMG within two months
Remain in the food colourants industry but internationalise the business	Prepare a shortlist of possible overseas locations for both production and R&D purposes	Three months
	Appoint a leading Director of International Operations to the KMG, from outside BWF, to champion this change	Six months to appointment, but start the process now
Acquire other specialist food ingredients businesses	First, the KMG should agree on the characteristics of suitable acquisitions (products, size, locations, etc.)	Two months
	Prepare a potential list of acquisitions that meet those criteria for more detailed review	6 to 9 months
Aggressively expand R&D	Agree a revised budget for R&D	Two months
	Look at ways in which this can be spent – look for ideas from, but not limited to, existing R&D department – may include much increased collaboration with both local and overseas universities	Four months

BWF Case – Exercise 4: Suggested Solution

Elements of the Medium-term Business Plan for Black & White Foods

Prepared by Financial Analyst, ACA

I have set out below the actions that BWF will need to take as part of a medium-term business plan for the company:

- Review our financing needs and approach the bank with a revised financing plan – see draft of Executive Summary of a business plan.
- Organise a formal programme of review of food trends in emerging markets – this can be partly done electronically via 'blogs' which is much cheaper and quicker.
- Monitor our pricing performance – particularly by analysing proposals lost to understand whether it was pricing and, if so, the extent of the gap.
- Carry out an analysis of the customers served by our competitors that are owned by larger food companies and try and establish are there likely to be any potential conflicts of interest that we can exploit.
- Put in place a cost containment/reduction plan.
- Develop enhanced testing methodologies for new products to respond to the need to get new products to market faster.
- Put in place a strict reporting methodology for all product or customer incidents so that KMG can respond immediately.
- Systematically try to increase the international background of our staff.
- Set a five-year R&D budget.
- Develop an incentive plan for key staff.
- Set up an R&D facility overseas.
- Develop an explicit policy to protect against potential conflicts of interest with different customers.
- Publicise our successes in the past with partnership-type arrangements.
- Stress importance of participation in partnership-type arrangements to staff as part of performance review process.
- Develop a programme of looking at Quality Control in other industries to look for best in class initiatives.
- Develop a contingency plan to kick in if QC problems do occur.
- Prepare a shortlist of possible overseas locations for both production and R&D purposes, and progress through to end decision on both.
- Appoint a leading Director of International Operations to the KMG, from outside BWF, to champion the internationalisation of the business.
- Agree on suitable characteristics for potential acquisitions of other specialist food ingredients companies.
- Prepare a potential list of acquisitions.
- Develop an enhanced R&D plan.

I have drafted the following suggested Executive Summary for a Business Plan suitable for finance raising:

Black and White Foods Limited (BWF) is a major Irish company and one of the five largest food colourant businesses in the world with turnover of €/£220 million, with minimal borrowings and many of the largest food customers in the world as customers. X Venture Capital are 20% shareholders in BWF. There is consistent and growing demand for our products, based on our own proprietary research, consistently keeping us ahead of our competitors. The market for our products is worldwide and growing well ahead of general economic growth, as there is significant growth in Home Meal Replacement eating as economies worldwide become more developed. Edible colourants are a critical factor in the appearance of processed food, yet form only a tiny part of the overall cost of the product, meaning less price pressure from BWF customers. BWF have many competitors, but as one of the five largest such food colourant companies in the world we are in a strong competitive position.

BWF has a well-established key management team of 20 people and is not overly dependant on any one person. Our strategy is to continue to focus on what we know best and where we are strongest – edible food colourants, which is a worldwide and growing market. Over the next five years we intend to further internationalise our business, establishing R&D and production centres outside Ireland. Over this five-year period we expect to earn cumulative EBIDTA of €/£ x millions, but will require initial borrowings of €/$z to make these investments, which we expect to fully repay within N years of drawdown.

BWF Case – Exercise 5: Suggested Solution

Review of the Current Organisational Model of Black & White Foods

Prepared by Financial Analyst, ACA

The strengths of the current functional organisational model employed by BWF are as follows:

- The current model has clearly worked well in the past.
- The functional model is clearly understood globally and it helps people know what they need to do and where they stand in the organisation.
- The idea of having a deputy for all functional heads is good.
- The regular pattern of meetings means that decisions can be made and followed up promptly.
- Promotion from within produces loyal and knowledgeable top executives.
- The cautious culture of the company has worked well to date.
- It is good that all major functions in the business have access to senior management.

The weaknesses of the current functional organisational model employed by BWF are as follows:

- There is no formal organisational chart which means that people may be unclear as to their roles and to whom they report.
- The KMG has too many people on it – 20 is too large a group to be ideal – witness the inability to draft a mission statement.
- The KMG is not international enough and that will have to change if BWF wishes to become a truly international company.
- The danger of promotion from within is that it tends to produce insular thinking without a willingness to learn from outsiders.
- There are family members involved in management and this will always run the risk of promotion on blood ties rather than merit, which can also act as a disincentive for good non-family members to make a career in the company.
- There are no non-executive directors so corporate governance is poor.
- The danger of meeting so often is that there is not sufficient time to fully consider major issues.
- The span of control for Jim Stanley is too wide, with eight direct reports.
- Most of the KMG deals with operational matters, whereas the highest decision-making unit in the company should be focused on strategy formulation, implementation and analysis.

The changes that should be made to the organisational structure are as follows:

- A board of directors should be put in place above the KMG – the board should comply with the UK Code on Corporate Governance and contain a representative of the venture capitalists.
- This Board should meet monthly.
- There should be Audit, Nomination and Remuneration Committees.
- The KMG can continue below this Board.
- The number of direct reports to Jim Stanley should be reduced to four – Finance, International, R&D, Operations.
- An external high-calibre director of international operations should be appointed from outside the company.
- A formal organisation chart should be developed.